ASTROLOGY
AND · THE
SPIRITUAL PATH

ASTROLOGY
AND · THE
SPIRITUAL PATH

T·H·E
SPIRITUAL
SIGNIFICANCE
O·F
AGE
PROGRESSION

BRUNO & LOUISE HUBER

SAMUEL WEISER, INC.
York Beach, Maine

First published in English in 1990 by
Samuel Weiser, Inc.
PO Box 612
York Beach, Maine 03910

Library of Congress Cataloging-in-Publication Data

Huber, Bruno.
    [Lebensuhr im Horoskop. Band 3. English]
    Astrology and the spiritual path : the spiritual significance
of age progression / Bruno and Louise Huber.
    Translation of: Lebensuhr im Horoskop, Bd. 3.
    1. Horoscopes. 2. Progressions (Astrology) 3. Age
(Psychology) — Miscellanea. 4. Life cycle, Human —
Miscellanea. 5. Spiritual life — Miscellanea. I. Huber,
Louise. II. Title.
BF1728.A2H82 1990
133.5'4 — dc20   89-77692
                                                                  CIP

ISBN 0-87728-706-6

Cover painting entitled "In the Beginning" ©Rob Schouten,
1990

Typeset in 10 Baskerville by
Sans Serif, Inc.
Printed in the United States of America

CONTENTS

Part One: Psychological Dimensions

Part Two: The Spiritual Path

Appendix

LIST OF COLOR PLATES

Planetary Symbols

Sun	☉		♂	Mars
Moon	☾		♃	Jupiter
Saturn	♄		♅ (⛢)	Uranus
Mercury	☿		♆	Neptune
Venus	♀		♇ (♇)	Pluto
Moon's ascending node	☊			

Zodiac Symbols

Aries	♈		♎	Libra
Taurus	♉		♏	Scorpio
Gemini	♊		♐	Sagittarius
Cancer	♋		♑	Capricorn
Leo	♌		♒	Aquarius
Virgo	♍		♓	Pisces

Dear Reader,

We hope that this book will provide guidance in your present period of change. Many people have experienced spiritual crisis and need help—mostly in the form of understanding, encouragement and support. Our earnest wish is that what you read here will provide you with this sort of help. When you apply Age Progression to your horoscope in the light of what has happened to you in life, you should be able to discover if past or present problems relate to a conflict between character and conduct, to an expansion of consciousness, to spiritual growth, or simply to teething troubles of the psyche.

In this third volume, we deal with various causes of psychological problems, and suggest ways of using the horoscope to penetrate to the core of these problems. You will see that quite often knowing that personal evolution is taking place is enough to bring you back into harmony with the laws of nature and with yourself.

May this book give new insights, a desire for further spiritual development and, where it is missing, a positive attitude to life.

Bruno and Louise Huber

ASTROLOGY
AND · THE
SPIRITUAL PATH

To be free of all authority, of your own and that of another, is to die to everything of yesterday, so that your mind is always fresh, always young, innocent, full of vigour and passion. It is only in this state that one learns and observes. And for this a great deal of awareness is required, actual awareness of what is going on inside yourself . . .

Jiddu Krishnamurti
Freedom From the Known

Part One

PSYCHOLOGICAL DIMENSIONS

Chapter One

The Zodiac in Color:
Life From Red Through Violet

I t may seem surprising that we are beginning this discussion by using the color circle in our study of the spiritual meaning of Age Progression. However, there is a good reason for this: the color spectrum (the rainbow), when laid round the horoscope, gives a picture of personal development very similar to that given by the theory of Age Progression; it also expresses the same life cycle idea. A rainbow spanning the sky may be viewed as a bridge, or heavenly gateway, symbolizing high spiritual advancement. The law of development — of evolution even — lies within it.

The rainbow is a very impressive natural phenomenon. Most of us have gazed in wonder at this bright arch springing out of nothingness; and we are also familiar with the bands of concentric colors (red, orange, yellow, green, blue, violet) produced when a light source shines on a glass prism or on a drop of water. Now, the Age Point is comparable to a light source, and radiates like a sun from the central circle of the astrological chart. As it travels through the chart, it "lights up" the planets,

signs and houses in many ways. These changes can be symbolized by color, and this is why we work with color in the chart.
See color Plate 1 on page 97.

The Color Spectrum

Various attempts were made by astrologers to assign colors to
zodiacal signs and planets, but not in connection with the spectrum until Bruno Huber compared the color circle with the
course of life through the houses. The results are astounding;
but, before discussing them, we must explain what we mean by
the color spectrum.

The spectrum, also known as the rainbow phenomenon, is
the splitting of a beam of white light into various colors. This
happens either through the refraction of light in a prism or
through diffraction. White sunlight is actually composed of
bright colors — the spectral colors. A distinction is made
between the three primaries, red, yellow and blue, and the
three secondaries, orange, green and violet, plus all the intermediate shades, as well as the invisible infrared and ultraviolet.
The latter lie just beyond the red and violet ends of the spectrum respectively.

The spectrum can be explained scientifically and its colors
have been carefully number-tagged. The light perceived by the
human eye consists of the visible part of the spectrum with
wavelengths varying from 4000 (violet) through 7600 (red)
Ångström units. Since the spectrum is continuous it contains
innumerable tints, not just what are popularly known as "the
seven colors of the rainbow." People with good vision can distinguish between 2,000 and 10,000 shades of color.

Astrological Colors

In Plate 1 you will see a circle of color inside the zodiac and the houses. The spectrum used is an ordinary continuous spectrum. For convenience of reference, we have listed certain wavelengths at regular intervals. The spectrum, which in reality would be straight, has been curved round the zodiac in such a way that it begins and ends at 0° Aries (or the Ascendant). The color circle formed in this way can readily be compared with the path of life. There has been no distortion by stretching some parts of the spectrum and squeezing others; on the contrary, the prismatic spacing of the colors has been faithfully preserved.

To make it conform to current theory, the spectrum has often been pulled out of shape (a crime perpetrated for a long time in the art world); the underlying assumption being that opposite colors in a color wheel are bound to be "complementaries" giving white or black when mixed. This assumption is not founded in fact, because pure black is virtually non-existent; that is to say, by chopping the spectrum into equal sections, one is never going to obtain the ingredients of pure black. Nearly all mixtures reveal some hue or other, as we see for example in the browns or dark greys.

In our philosophic moments, we have an inveterate tendency to think in terms of black and white. The force of our logic compels us to see polar opposites as stark contrasts. This is a human fixation, and has nothing to do with the natural world where things are not simply black or white. On examining the color circle, we should let nature correct us and begin to allow our ideas to agree with reality.

The Three Primary Colors

The spectrum contains three primary colors that are recognized by physics. These are pure red, yellow, and indigo (or deep blue). These three primaries are very important: in the spectrum they blend with one another in varying proportions to give an infinity of intermediate shades. As indicated by the small inner arcs in our horoscope color circle, red extends more than 180° (in fact for ca. 210°) from Aquarius through the beginning of Virgo, yellow extends even further and traverses eight signs from Taurus through Sagittarius (ca. 240°), and blue, which starts in the lemon-yellow region, extends from Scorpio through Pisces (ca. 150°).

It is interesting that yellow occupies the most space. On surveying the complete circle, we observe that it is also the lightest color. It is more dazzling than blue or red. This ties in with the fact that we have a yellow sun — even though we may see it as white. A glance at the chart will show pure yellow at 5800 Å. The surface temperature of the Sun is 5800°, so it is not a white star but a yellow one.

By the law of analogy, the three primary colors of the spectrum correspond to the three-part division of the horoscope already described in Volume 1 of *Life Clock*.[1] This being so, we are in a position to evaluate the Age Progression colors qualitatively.

Red = 1st third = Houses 1–4
Color of manifestation, purposeful, dynamic movement.

Yellow = 2nd third = Houses 5–8
Color of contact, attitude, urge to make relationships.

---

[1]Bruno and Louise Huber, *Lifeclock: Age Progression in the Horoscope, Vol 1* (York Beach, ME: Samuel Weiser, 1982).

Blue = 3rd third = Houses 9–12
Color of retreat, self-orientation, peace, isolation.

Psychological Effect of Colors

The psychological effect of colors, or color psychology, is a field
that has already gathered a great deal of interesting data. The
subjective meaning of color was appreciated by Goethe[2] many
years ago; and he wrote at length against the rather matter-of-
fact physics of Newton,[3] who was the first to make a detailed
scientific investigation of light and color. Ostwald and Müller[4]
can be regarded as modern creators of the color wheel,[5] which
still has an appreciable number of devotees in the art world and
may be seen in the complementary color wheels illustrated by
Itten and Grob. Following the Pythagorean tradition, Kaiser
linked color with mathematical and musical studies, while the
painter Kandinsky was enabled by his artistic sensitivity to
produce one of the most psychologically valuable contributions
to color theory that have so far appeared. Finally, the psycholo-
gist Lüscher[6] developed a color test that seems to be appreciated more by the public than by the professionals. It is fairly
well known that colors can affect people's moods. For example,
green has a calming influence, red rouses one to be active and

---

[2]J. W. Goethe, *Essays on Art and Literature* (New York: Suhrkamp, 1980). In
addition to the list of Goethe's writings mentioned in the Bibliography, see
also *Goethe's Color Theory*, Rupprecht Mattaei, ed., and Herb Aach, ed. and tr.
Published simultaneously in 1971 by Reinhold, New York, and Studio Vista,
London.

[3]Isaak Newton, *Opticks* (New York: Dover, 1952).

[4]See the bibliography for works by Wilhelm Ostwald and Aemilius Muller.

[5]*The Rainbow* (Boston: Shambhala, 1975) reprints color wheels by Newton
(1706), Goethe (1792), Chevreul (1839), and other famous theoreticians
earlier than Ostwald, whose anno 1916 wheel is also given. *Tr.*

[6]See the Bibliography for references to works by Johannes Itten, Walter
Oscar Grob, Wassily Kandinsky, and Max Luscher.

enterprising, yellow imparts a sense of warmth and a desire to make contacts. Dull and faded colors easily lead to depression and melancholy. Lively colors help to make work a pleasure, but colors that are too glaring break concentration. Findings like these have been utilized to some extent by physicians and teachers, but most of all by industrial psychologists. For instance, a person whose favorite color is yellow will not look at life in the same way as a person who prefers red or blue. Lovers of red are very thrusting and egocentric, and often ruthless (1st third); lovers of yellow are intensely contact-orientated and therefore dependent on their environment (2nd third); lovers of blue are fairly passive, upward looking and spiritually minded. These are fundamentally different attitudes to life, and it might be a good idea to consider the effects of the three primary colors in more detail.

Red

Red strives to develop and to spread beyond its natural borders. It represents a love of life, the survival instinct common to us all even in childhood. This will is a primary urge, an inherent activity; and psychologically it is embodied in a dynamic restlessness that continually presses forward, although occasionally it amounts to nothing more than movement for movement's sake.

Yellow

Yellow is the chief color in our solar system, because we have a yellow sun. It is the contact color and is important to men and women as social beings. As a contact color, yellow induces people to approach each other to give or ask favors; under its influence, they agree with one another, grow attached, and form alliances. In other words, relationships of all kinds are the province of yellow. Such relationships can be based on practical considerations, or on personal affinity, as in erotic or platonic friendships. Yellow can signify harmonious companionship with give and take, but also exploitation and endless demands. Yellow is our most important color, since it is the contact color, and without contact human beings cannot live. "No man is an island," and, after a while, seclusion becomes unpleasant and even unbearable. We are social animals and the urge signified by yellow is remarkably strong in us. The move toward community life, toward union with You, toward synthesis and oneness, is mysteriously connected with our yellow sun.

Blue

Blue is diametrically opposed to red in quality. Whereas red — to some extent — bends us to the earth, blue lifts us from the earth and removes us from mundane existence. We feel something of what space travellers must feel as they watch our planet vanish. As it recedes, so does everything gross and earthbound. We return to the self. Breaking free from the material, we enter another and spiritual dimension. So transcendental blue corresponds to retiringness: we want to be on our own, to be left in peace, to enjoy solitude, to distance ourselves from the world and the things of the world.

It seems that each one of us has "three people" inside him or her. The first simply desires to live (red), the second seeks encounters (yellow), and the third returns to itself (blue). However, we must not forget the secondary colors, which have their own significance in Age Progression.

The Three Secondary Colors

These arise from the three primaries.

Orange

This is a mixture of red and yellow. Key words are penetration, extroverted contact-making, erotic and aggressive behavior.

Green

This is a mixture of yellow and blue. Green relates to desire for protection, self-control, reserve.

Violet

This is blue and red mixed together. Key words are transcendence, dreams, unreality, innocence.

These tints are always a mixture of two primary colors. What is more, all other tints in the spectrum arise through a proportioned mixture of two primaries. If we begin with lemon yellow, for example, we find a high percentage of yellow with only a trace of blue, but enough to make the yellow cool. With the addition of a little more blue, the yellow darkens to light green, lime green, etc. As the blue increases and the yellow decreases, the greenness becomes more pronounced until blue predominates to give blue-green (malachite green). Finally blue takes over and yellow completely disappears. Between the pure color points lie the half-color points, where there is a fifty-fifty mixture of the two colors. The orange half-color point is at the cusp of the 5th house. Somewhere near cusp 9 is the green half-color point, and just before the Ascendant is the purple half-color point. The arc from the pure red point (carmine) to the yellow point subtends an angle of 150° (quincunx); from yellow to blue (indigo) we have a trine and from blue back to red we have a square aspect. This means that the measured distances between the pure color points are not equal. The configuration is a dominant triangle containing three distinct aspects. Psychologically speaking, it is a dynamic structure signifying growth or learning. As we see, nature is not symmetrical; a grant trine would have been symmetrical. Thinkers of the past always sought for symmetry, because for them it represented absolute purity or perfection, but nature is in fact assymetrical and therefore dynamic.

Turning now to the half-color points on our circle, we discover that they are spaced symmetrically — they form a grand trine. But here we are dealing with color mixtures, colors of the second order, and no longer with pure colors. Symmetry does not appear until we come to colors of the second order.

The Color Circle as a Life Clock

The experimental meaning of the colors follows their distribution by the light spectrum through the house system. As we know, people in the same age group have much in common in regard to attitude toward life, basic interests, and problems; they are colored the same, so to speak. On examining the color circle, we observe an interesting correspondence between the qualities of the colors and the course of life through the twelve houses. Our sequence of experiences in terms of color is very much the same as our sequence of experiences in terms of the movement of the Age Point through the house system.

Because, as the old adage says, the microcosm is like the macrocosm, the pattern of our lives must mimic that of the cosmos and of the spectrum. The zodiac belongs to the reality of the cosmos, the spectrum belongs to the reality of light, and the house system belongs to the reality of our lives. In the color circle, these three realities are welded into a functional whole. We exist within this circle. We grow, mature and die in it; and our self-expression is governed by its color changes. In the course of life we pass from pure red through more and more yellowy reds, pure yellow, various greens, blue, violet and finally purple.

Beginning and End

In the color circle, we have put the commencement of life at Aries in the zodiac and at the Ascendant in the house system. On the purple edge of the visible spectrum, life starts with the Ascendant, in dimness, before the dawn. The individual emerges from nothingness, from the invisible realm; and on the other side of the Ascendant he or she comes to the end of the journey. Life and death meet one another here. Now, if we try to make the spectrum "bite its own tail," we find that it does not quite manage it: there is a gap, an area of seeming nonexistence, separating the beginning (red) from the end (violet). At the junction of the spectral red and violet arises the mixed color purple, a color that is not spectral. It is not seen when white light is refracted by a glass prism because the spectrum apparently peters out. In reality the blue end of the spectrum is continued by an ultraviolet band, and the red by a band of infrared, although neither band is visible to us. There is something strangely significant about this, because the gap is like a gateway of incarnation through which the soul steps onto its life-path at red.

On the Ascendant life begins, and red is at the beginning too. It signifies our will to live, to manifest ourselves, to succeed, to be someone. The power of self-manifestation and self-assertion lies in red, which persists through the 5th house. In the 1st house, the self-motivated drive is expansive. Red is a highly active color, especially when mixed with yellow — which makes it even more intense and dynamic.

Yellow, the contact color, helps us to make contact with the You, also with whatever objects we encounter. Yellow stands at the You-point in the chart. As yellow comes more into the picture, there is a growing desire to press on in the yellow direction so as to find a You. When there is practically no yellow in the red, for example in the 2nd house, we are still more or less asocial, and refuse or hesitate to have anything to do with a You. Only at puberty does the longing for a You slowly make itself felt (3rd house). Probably we start thinking of ways and means of meeting a partner. Success has to wait until we are properly in the yellow phase. Then we enjoy ardent contact with the You — until the color blue steals in to cool things off a little.

Blue begins in the 8th house, with the need to break free from mundane affairs in order to be ourselves once more. The blue sector gives us knowledge of what we are like when not shackled by the bonds and obligations of the lower houses; it bestows a freedom and an independence that are uniquely an upper house experience. Blue characterizes the phase of withdrawal; perhaps that is why Goethe termed it spiritual. Although not entirely so, it does denote a certain aloofness from the duties and cares of everyday living (11th and 12th houses). It signifies retirement from the world and a turning toward the higher life. Blue is the color of detachment, self-knowledge and individuation in a loftier context. It is inherently restful, and gives us an opportunity to identify with the greater Whole.

Pure blue symbolizes infinity. The night sky verges on pure blue, especially before it is quite dark. If we avoid the horizon when gazing into the night sky, this blue will put us into a mystical frame of mind; in some countries, the twilight hour is also known as the blue hour (*blaue Stunde, l'heure bleu*).

Purple

The reader will readily work out the effects of mixtures of primary colors. However, one or two points are worth mentioning here. One of the most intriguing of the secondaries is the color opposite yellow, namely purple. This color is not contained in the visible spectrum, which becomes black at its red and violet ends; in fact the blackness contains infrared and ultraviolet radiation. Purple overlaps the Ascendant, which symbolizes the start and close of life. There is an underlying logic in this.

Purple is a color consisting of a fifty-fifty mixture of red and blue. It is a special color. Who wears purple? Ecclesiatical dignitaries, kings and emperors — in other words, those who are over everyone or who stand apart from everyone. A king is untouchable, beyond the reach of many things affecting ordinary mortals; so is a cardinal. Because ordinary human standards do not apply to them, they dress in purple.

Purple and violet (corresponding to the 12th house) are associated with nothingness in color psychology; violet in drawings or paintings has a zero function, showing something nonexistent or so transparent as to be intangible. Purple might be called an unreal color, it is not in the spectrum. A more understandable effect of purple is illusion. In the drawings of the mentally ill this color occurs quite frequently, because these people exist in an illusory and non-existent world. Color psychology regards purple as indicating an unreal state of mind in which the person concerned lives with at least part of his or her being somewhere that is "not of this world," in a fantasy world. When we find a planet at the zero point of the zodiac (0° Aries), the planet has something of this quality; what it represents is not fully incarnated; part remains "on the other side." Students who wish to go more deeply into the study of color should see the Bibliography for the most important books on the subject.

Chapter Two

The Influence of Temperament and Environment: The House Chart

The house chart is relatively new in astrology. Developed by Bruno Huber after years of psychological research, today it is a significant astro-psychological key to the study of human behavior. Earlier this century, astrologers like Pöllner spoke of the so-called mundane aspects or aspects made by planets to house cusps, the angles of which were calculated according to some house degree system. These aspects were used exclusively for event calculation. This was a first approach to our own type of mundane horoscope, in which the chart is adjusted so that the houses are all 30 degrees.

Today the house chart is employed as an ancillary diagnostic tool and provides valuable information about the total resources of the individual. It is a revolutionary method for the practitioner who wishes to establish the strength of impressions made by the environment — in other words, the behavior patterns that have been acquired by or imposed on the native. At times this house horoscope is quite unlike the radix, and the native's inner and outer lives are at odds with one another. In such cases, whereas the radix shows what is experienced as inner reality, the house horoscope shows a very different, essentially alien, outer reality. The misalignment between the internal and external worlds is clear. Detailed investigations have revealed that this misalignment is often the hidden cause of behavioral disorders, diseases and impaired development. The realization that we are living exclusively in the house horoscope and are behaving as we have been conditioned to behave, often without giving it a second thought, can produce a great shock and led to a freeing process.

Strictly speaking, the house chart is not new, but is derived from the radix mathematically to present another point of view[1]. In the mundane horoscope we look at the native from the outside (the houses are like aerials tuning in to the environment), while in the radix we look at the native from the inside. The abilities with which one is born are indicated by the positions of the planets in the zodiac. Now, just as twelve 30° signs are the units of measurement in the radix, so in the house chart twelve 30° houses perform the same function. Each radical house is adjusted to 30°, and the sizes of the signs and the distances between the planets become proportionally bigger or smaller than they are in the radix. See Plate 2 on page 98.

When turning to Plate 2, you will observe that the signs are stretched or compressed, and yet the size of a given sign in a given house remains the same and the planets keep their relative positions in the houses. However, new aspects are formed: the Moon, Saturn, Venus, and Mars each stand about the same distance in front of the new house cusps (ca. 2 to 3 house degrees) and are therefore aspecting one another, although they are in quite different zodiac degrees (Moon 2°

---

[1]The calculations of the house chart are not hard to do. You can learn it through a correspondence course offered through the English Huber School of Astrological Counselling, P.O. Box 9, Totnes, Devon TQ9 SYN, England. In the CORTEX computer program (API computer), the house positions of the planets and size of the signs are given in addition to their zodiac positions.

Aquarius, Saturn 10° Pisces, Venus 9° Virgo, Mars 22°
Libra). In house degrees, the Invert Point works out at
11°27'36" and the Low Point at 18°32'24" from the house
cusps. Experience shows that, in the house horoscope, the
aspects of the Age Point are most intense when it is at house
cusps and Low Points. In the radix, these are at the same
degrees, so there is a "double action." An example will make
this clearer. We discussed a chart in Volume 2 of *Lifeclock*[2]
which we will work with again. See figure 1 on page 18. In
what follows, we shall describe this chart and the house chart
derived from it.

On examination, it is immediately apparent that the
aspect configuration in the house chart is not the same as it is in
the radix — it has shrunk. This means that as a child, the native
failed to gain a proper understanding of her surroundings,
which played a "reduced" part in her development. Uranus
stands alone; it is no longer aspected as in the radix. Probably
the child was given no spiritual perspectives — such matters
were apparently never brought to her attention.

The Moon, the juvenile ego, is trine Mars and quincunx
Venus/Neptune in the house horoscope. And Saturn aspects
the Moon, which it does not do in the radix. As stated in
Lifeclock, V2, an Age Point transit of Saturn in the 5th year of
life coincided with a traumatic event that left a permanent scar
on the little girl's ego and later influenced her attitude about
love. There were some early sexual games with a neighbor's
boy; the mother caught and scolded her, and the father hit her
for the first time. She could not understand why her parents
were so upset. Nothing she had done before had been wrong in
their eyes. The attendant psychic impression produced bewil-
derment, fear of punishment, guilt feelings, mistrust of the
opposite sex, and sexual inhibition. Until she was 42, her

---

[2]Bruno and Louise Huber, *Lifeclock Volume 2: Practical Techniques for Counseling
Age Progression in the Horoscope* (York Beach, ME: Samuel Weiser, 1986).

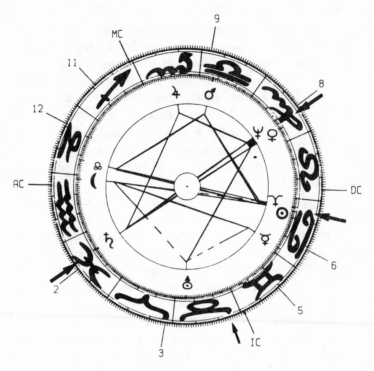

Figure 1.   Horoscope of a female client born July 16, 1935, at 20h45m, in Herisan, Switzerland.

mother was able to take advantage of this sense of shame to tie the daughter to her apron strings.

It is not possible to see from the radix alone why this experience made such a deep and lasting impression. Only the house chart shows how the young psyche could be so gravely wounded. The "house" aspects of the Moon and Saturn were very intense; therefore the Age Point was able to trigger the release of considerable latent energy. The Moon and Saturn are in semisextile and so are the libido planets Mars and Venus. These, together with Neptune, form a so-called "buffer figure," but solely in the house chart. What is more, we find that a T-square is formed between the Sun/Pluto conjunction in opposition to the north node and squared by Mars in the radix and by Jupiter in the house chart. Mars is being replaced by Jupiter. This represents the false impression that was made on the girl's mind, and the wrong attitude associated with guilt feelings from which she was unable to free herself until she was 42, at which time the "normal" Age Point reached the opposition to Saturn on the cusp of the 8th house, and the Neptune/ Venus sextile to Jupiter was activated in the radix, bringing a more natural understanding of sexuality.

As we see, working with the house horoscope combines techniques and provides additional understanding. This example may stimulate the reader to carry out personal research.

The Local Horoscope

The local horoscope is a new and valuable addition to the armory of modern and future astrologers. The world has become so small that, at some time during our lives, many of us will travel quite far and may change residences often. Now, each place has its own house system, its own environment. In a local horoscope the native's personal planets, sign positions and aspects are transferred to the house system of some place in which he or she once lived, is living now, or is thinking of living.

Perhaps the reader has sometimes wondered why one place is more congenial than another. The reason could be the collective environmental quality of the locality. For each region — astrologically speaking — has its own house system based on a zodiac inscribed on the earth's surface. Figure 2 on page 20 shows the house system for Zurich. Experience has

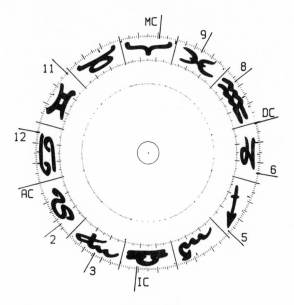

Figure 2.   Local houses for Zurich, Switzerland.

shown that the global system of coordinates with Greenwich as origin that was introduced at the end of the last century actually has a terrestrial zodiac as its basis—even though to all appearances it is a human invention!

Tests made by various modern astrologers on local ascendants and local meridians have demonstrated that the course of events at any given place is influenced by transits of the corresponding degrees of the zodiac. Our own researches have brought further facts to light. Each locality has not only an Ascendant and a Meridian but a whole house system. And the planets and signs in a person's chart are just as much influenced by this house system as events are!

Planets transferred from a birth chart to a local chart may well be brought to a more favorable house or to a more favorable position in their old house. There are many possible arrangements giving increased vitality or otherwise as the case may be. The local horoscope indicates how the native feels in a collective environment.

Horoscope Description

The local horoscope is relatively new in astrology. We have not yet been able to gather a great deal of data on interpretation and on the Age Point. Figure 3 on page 22 is an example of how the local horoscope can enhance the understanding of the radix. Anyone who wants to do some research for themselves will find this example useful. We have chosen this horoscope because we know the individual well. In describing the local horoscope we shall concentrate on the three personality planets — Sun, Saturn, and the Moon. These are decisive for self-development and for a sense of well-being in a place.

The Sun is posited in the birth chart just after the cusp of the 2nd house; in the local horoscope of Zurich, however, it lies in the shadow of the 11th house. And so the symbol of self-awareness moves from the lower to the upper half of the horoscope. In Zurich this lady had better opportunities for individuation and self-realization than in her birthplace. The position of the Sun shows that she was challenged by what was going on around her in Zurich to sharpen her identity and to perform a definite function in concert with like-minded people. Solving the various problems that arose was not easy: the Sun stands in the shadow of the cusp and therefore inside a stress zone; what is more, it is in the intercepted sign of Taurus, which has no house cusp of its own. More effort is required from shadow planets; and intercepted signs speak of inappropriate reactions to an environment that is not properly perceived and from which the native gets poor feedback. In the radix, the Sun in the 2nd house shows that the native's material resources had to be fully exploited and that she had to shoulder the responsibil-

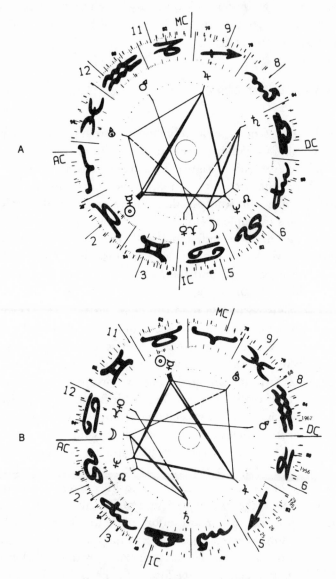

Figure 3.   (A) Radix for a female born May 10, 1924, 03h15. Details of the birthplace have been withheld for confidentiality. (B) The local horoscope of Zurich.

ity for her finances. She herself had to procure whatever was necessary to bring her plans to fruition.

Saturn moves from the radical 7th house to the local 4th house, that is to say from the upper to the lower half of the horoscope. In the 4th house, Saturn is usually experienced as stress or pressure from the environmental group. The native was always afraid that the neighbors were going to take offense at something or other. She always had to be doing things for the family, for the home, for those around; she felt tied, and responsible for everything that had happened or might happen, and she tried to prepare for all eventualities. Since radical Saturn is in the 7th house, she wanted support from her partner, but little help was forthcoming from that direction; certainly not as much as previously (square to the Moon).

The Moon moves from the radical 5th house to just in front of the local horoscope Ascendant. Emotional rapport with the place was important to her health. The Cancerian Moon at the AC reacted subjectively to acceptance and also to the slightest rejection; the native was always tense, and uncertain whether or not she was making a good impression. The worry drained her of energy. She quickly senses sympathy or antipathy, and had a hard fight against unjustified fears (shadow planet = tendency to compensate).

The Age Point in the Local Horoscope

It goes without saying that an Age Point travels through the houses of the local horoscope; but in these the AP reveals outer stimuli, not the fundamental inner vibrations revealed by the radix. The AP registers the influence of the locality and of the local community, and the native's probable reactions to these may be inferred. The method is the same as with the normal Age Point. We look in the local horoscope for the period in which we are interested. The path of the local Age Point starts at birth, but we do not join it until the point in time when the native changed residence. From then on it shows what events and opportunities are likely in the new home — often more clearly and with more accurate timing than the radical AP does. To assess the course of life, we track the local Age Point as it aspects the planets in the local horoscope. The significance of these individuals aspects can be found in *Life Clock Volume 2*.

In our example, the lady arrived in Zurich for the first time in September, 1952. The local Age Point was at 20° Sagittarius, thus exactly at the galactic center — suggesting that the visit was going to have something to do with universal values. In October, 1952, the native received a proposal of marriage under the sextile to Saturn and quincunx to the Moon. In February, 1953, she finally settled in Zurich. The local Age Point was at 28° Sagittarius trine to the Dragon's Head — so this was an important event for her personal development and spiritual task. The marriage is not indicated by the local AP. However, it was solemnized in March, 1953, when the AP was exactly conjunct Neptune in the birth chart.

From February, 1954, to October, 1955, the local Age Point was in opposition to Venus and Pluto. This was an intensely critical period as far as decision-making was concerned; and, in August, 1956, when the AP was at IP 6, the native left Zurich in order to take up spiritual work full time (opposition Pluto). In September, 1962, when the local Age Point was exactly conjunct Mars, she returned to Zurich. Her absences had lasted from IP 6 through IP 7, that is to say, it practically coincided with the gap between Jupiter and Mars in the local horoscope. In December, 1964, at the opposition to Neptune, she started her own service enterprise in the vicinity of Zurich. March, 1968 found her launching a Uranian-type project. At this very time, the local Age Point entered Pisces, where Uranus was waiting. The preparatory work had already been taken in hand in September, 1967, at the opposition to the north node. This was the prelude to intense personal and mental activity. There is an interesting connection here with the aspect cycles (see *Life Clock, Volume 1*).[3] At the trine to the Dragon's Head she came to Zurich. At the opposition she was busy laying the foundations for what was to follow. With the transit of Uranus she set herself up as an independent (9th house) lecturer on esoteric subjects. As her skill improved in this direction, she proceeded to form and lead her own group. Uranus in the radical 12th house shows that even in her old home she liked researching spiritual and hidden things.

During the passage through the 10th house of the local horoscope, success attended all her professional and spiritual endeavors. From 1978 onwards she began to attract attention, her popularity grew and people took her work seriously. In particular, honors came her way and her efforts received increased recognition when the Sun was transited (even though it is in an intercepted sign). Her self-confidence and self-assurance blossomed and she achieved the financial stability for which she had struggled so long—a vindication of the radical Sun's presence on the 2nd cusp.

Discrepancy Between Temperament and Environment in Signs and Houses

Another new approach in astrological psychology is the confrontation of signs and houses in order to reveal the interplay between temperament and environment. This facet of psychological interpretation is so important that we have decided, in spite of is complexity, to discuss its bearing on Age Progres-

---

[3]Bruno and Louise Huber, *Lifeclock Volume 1: Age Progression in the Horoscope* (York Beach, ME: Samuel Weiser, 1982).

sion. Further information is available in the self-instruction manual "Development Processes in the Horoscope."[4]

It is a known fact that besides the natural tendencies shown in the radix there are influences that impinge on us from the environment. Therefore, when judging the horoscope, especially the progressed horoscope, we need to discover where disposition and conditioning (signs and houses) are at odds with one another; only so can human problems — not the least our own — be properly assessed. By applying the Age Progression method, we can determine how much the development of our natural inclinations and abilities is helped or hindered by the structure of our environment. This is revealed by the arrangement of the signs and houses, by their relative displacement in regard to one another, and by the planetary positions. As we compare the house system with the zodiac, we see exactly where the inner self is in accord with the concrete life situation, with our milieu, and where it is not. To elaborate a little, consider the following:

1) *The house system* symbolizes both the environment and our adjustment to it. It shows the effect of background and upbringing, the way in which we respond to or have been conditioned by our surroundings.

2) *The zodiac* indicates our natural disposition, our own contribution to life. What is more, hereditary factors can be identified from the positions of the planets in the signs.

3) *The planetary positions* in the signs, together with the aspect structure, also depict our natural disposition; however, it is necessary to observe that the aspect structure expresses a deeplying life motivation that is not wholly and absolutely explicable in terms of inherited characteristics.

---

[4]Louise Huber, *Entwicklungsprozesse im Horoskop.* (Adliswil, Switzerland: Astrologisch-Psychologisches Institute, 1980). Further information is also available through the English Huber School.

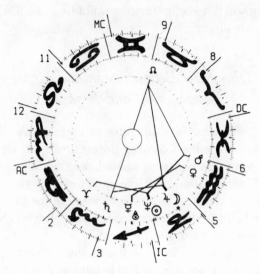

Figure 4. Virgo on the Ascendant changes the position of the sign Capricorn from its natural house position (the 10th) into the 4th.

In almost every horoscope, the zodiac is out of alignment with the house system to some degree. This is obvious from the fact that charts have different rising signs, and that it is not usual for 0° Aries to be on the Ascendant. The lack of alignment mirrors a friction or tension between the true nature of the individual and the conditioning produced by force of circumstances. It signifies a certain path of development. If, for example, Virgo is on the Ascendant, the zodiac is, so to speak, reversed in the house system. Capricorn, which really belongs to the highest point (i.e., the 10th house) is now at the lowest (the 4th). See figure 4.

If the Sun, which is strongest at the MC, stands in the lower half (the so-called collective area) of the horoscope, there will not likely be a self-confident expression of the true nature, but the conditioning and inhibition that relate to the lower-half house in which the Sun is posited. Very probably, the native's upbringing will not lead to the free unfolding of a distinct, self-reliant personality.

Differences Between Sign and House (Temperament and Behavior)

In working out what is happening in the native's life at any given time, we use the following procedure: first, we find the house the Age Point occupies; second, we find the sign it occupies; third, we see how well the qualities of sign and house agree with one another; and fourth, we note the aspects made by the Age Point to the planets in the radix. In this chapter we shall consider the third point in detail.

For interspersing the Age Point, the difference between sign and house (temperament and behavior) is very interesting and instructive. The house system reveals powerful outside forces that tie us up or push us in certain directions, or maybe aid our development. If we trace the AP through a particular house during a certain period in life, we shall be left in no doubt of the compatibility or incompatibility of sign and house. The sign quality is felt inwardly, causing us to know what we really want. At the same time we experience, through the house, what the world expects and requires of us. The two things can be quite different. The inner will is often contrary to the demands of the environment. The result is unnecessary reverses and apparent failures, as well as difficulties in adjustment with corresponding psychic crises. The latter can be avoided if we learn how to behave; in other words, what and what not to do.

First we need to know that the origin of most problems lies, not in our temperament, but in the conflict between our temperament and real life situations, i.e., between "what I want" and "what the world wants from me." This confrontation between will and obligation begets inner struggles and difficulties, but is also a tremendous powerhouse for development when put in operation by the passage of the Age Point through the houses.

The Age Point, our focus of consciousness, helps us to distinguish between the demands and opportunities of the environment and our own inner desires and aptitudes. In studying the house theme, we gain an insight into the best way to respond to what is happening around us — whether to go along with it, or to disengage from it because it does not meet our deepest desires. We shall learn something about our freedom when we can take a cold hard look at the clamoring world and then make a judicious, informed decision to give it some, all, or none of what it wants. If we are ignorant of this option, we more or less deliver ourselves up to suffer from "force of circumstances" or from the imposition of others; our dependence on stimuli, baits, opportunities, and commands being due to a lack of the concept of freedom.

So what can the horoscope tell us about the degree of freedom? To answer this, the first step is to discover how far the qualities of the sign and house agree; a point most easily determined by seeing whether or not they belong to the same cross or the same temperament. The second step is to assess the degree of agreement or disagreement, and to find out where we need to improve. As we already know from reading *Life Clock, Volume 1*, the cardinal, fixed and mutable crosses represent our motivations. To outline this concept once more very briefly:

Cross	Keyword	Law	Motivation
Cardinal	Impulse	Power	Conquest
Fixed	Perseverance	Economy	Protection
Mutable	Relationship	Love	Understanding

House/Sign Combinations in the Crosses

We shall now indicate a few of the possible combinations of the crosses. A detailed discussion would exceed the limits of this book. Figure 5 may help you understand this discussion.

Cardinal/Fixed

Fixed houses 2, 5, 8, 11
Cardinal signs: Aries, Cancer, Libra, Capricorn

When a cardinal sign lies in a fixed house, the cardinal and fixed principles form an obvious complementary pair. With this combination, we can be very productive and successful, especially when we make conscious use of the Age Point. If, for example, the cardinal sign *Libra is in the 5th house*, the typical contact-making, imposing behavior and self-promotion of Libra express with charm, adroitness and good taste.

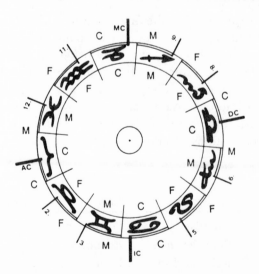

Figure 5. Cardinal (C), fixed (F), and mutable (M) combinations of house and sign.

Fixed/Cardinal
Cardinal houses 1, 4, 7, 10
Fixed signs: Taurus, Leo, Scorpio, Aquarius

When the roles are reversed, and a fixed sign is in a cardinal house, the two crosses are well able to complement one another. For instance, individuals with *Leo in the 10th house* can make a good impression. They usually know their own minds, and have no difficulty in striking an individual attitude. The demands of the 10th house are taken in stride, and no great adjustments are required when the Age Point passes through it.

Mutable/Fixed
Fixed houses 2, 5, 8, 11
Mutable signs: Gemini, Virgo, Sagittarius, Pisces

When a mutable sign is in a fixed house, motives are mixed. The sign favors change and novelty; the house favors stability and the tried and true. The result is internal strife: a conflict between desire and necessity that often becomes painfully obvious when the Age Point activates it. For instance, if *Sagittarius is in the 2nd house*, the Archer gives a love of liberty and of independence from material things which life seems loath to satisfy. In the 2nd, Taurean house, the Sagittarian nature is forced to concentrate on the accumulation of wealth before there is any possibility of living a free life. Often this goal is not achieved until the AP is in the opposing 8th house (ages 42–48).

Fixed/Mutable
Mutable houses 3, 6, 9, 12
Fixed signs: Taurus, Leo, Scorpio, Aquarius

With a fixed sign in a mutable house (e.g., *Scorpio in the 9th house*), desire is at odds with necessity (especially between ages

48 and 54), because the fixed, conservative principle has nothing in common with the fluctuating demands of the environment. This produces an unsettled frame of mind—in the 9th house regarding outlook on life, religious beliefs and inner orientation, and in the other mutable houses regarding their matters. The native has to learn that there is no such thing as ultimate safety, but life is an ongoing adventure.

Cardinal/Mutable
Mutable houses 3, 6, 9, 12
Cardinal signs: Aries, Cancer, Libra, Capricorn

When on the other hand, a cardinal sign occupies a mutable house, the principle of impulse goes well with the changing demands of the house, because there is very little conflict between the two crosses. If *Cancer is in the 6th house*, the efficiency of the native's work will generally depend on feelings of sympathy and antipathy. During the passage of the Age Point through this house, we should notice that we enjoy pleasant relationships with our colleagues. We work best in harmonious and agreeable surroundings.

Mutable/Cardinal
Cardinal houses 1, 4, 7, 10
Mutable signs: Gemini, Virgo, Sagittarius, Pisces

This combination, too, generally functions without much difficulty. For example, if *Virgo is in the 4th house*, the native could be a woman engaged in the important work of caring for a family. If so, she would make sure she got all the activity and change she wanted by going visiting, moving house frequently, taking trips, or constantly rearranging the rooms.

Chapter Three

The Age Point and the
Four Temperaments

Whereas the crosses represent our essential drive or motivations, the temperaments characterize the types and modes of our behavior, that is to say they characterize *how* we do things. In short: the three crosses answer the question why? and the four temperaments answer the question how?

The three qualities of the crosses manifest themselves individually in a regularly recurring series of temperaments. By combining the three crosses with the four temperaments we obtain the twelve signs of the zodiac. To understand the different effects or types of energy of the separate signs (and also of the houses), we can analyze them into their crosses and temperaments and interpret them both as primary principles and as combinations. (See also *Life Clock, Vol. 1*, pp. 142–152.)

In many books the four temperaments are also called elements. The latter are the building blocks of all material structures and organic tissues. Each element represents a basic type of energy and consciousness. When the Age Point changes

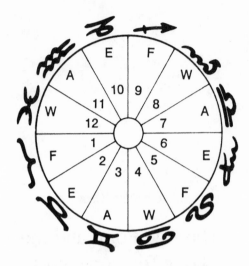

Figure 6.   The sign/house temperaments. A = Air, E = Earth, W = Water, and F = Fire.

from one sign to another, our temperament alters abruptly — often over night. As modern physics has shown, energy can be converted into mass; in much the same way, the four elements condense into material and psychic conditions, and crystallize into various characteristics or forms of behavior. What is more, they have a psychological connection with the four colors, red, green, yellow, blue, assigned to the four temperaments shown in our charts. See figure 6.

The four temperaments can be linked to the four states of aggregation of matter:

Color	The Four States of Aggregation		
Green	Earth	=	Solid
Blue	Water	=	Liquid
Yellow	Air	=	Gas
Red	Fire	=	Plasma

It is life that expresses itself as an organic whole through the four elements, adopts a certain hue or vibration, and changes our inner attitude accordingly. In describing the essential action of the elements, Stephen Arroyo says: "The birth chart therefore reveals your energy pattern, or cosmic attunement to the four elements. In other words, the chart shows the various vibratory manifestations that comprise the individual's expression in this plane of creation, all of which follow a specific pattern of order which the chart symbolizes. In scientific terms, the chart shows your 'energy field' or what clairvoyants call the 'aura.'"[1]

From an esoteric point of view, the elements correspond to the four subtle or fine-structure bodies of the human being. These interpenetrate one another and, taken as a whole, may be likened to a force-field that envelops the physical body and supplies it with life-giving energy. All four elements are present in each of us, even though individually we incline to one type more than another.

The element earth is a symbol of the physical body that binds us to real life, to the tangible world. The element fire corresponds to the vital or etheric body. This has a close connection with the physical body and provides the coarser substance of life. The element water is linked to the emotional or astral body, which is animated by subjective ideas, hopes and wishes. The element air is connected with the mental body, in which all thought forms are contained and into which new thoughts are continually pouring from the universal thought plane. The esoteric paradigm is as follows:

Physical body	Earth element
Etheric body	Fire element
Emotional body	Water element
Mental body	Air element

---

[1]Stephen Arroyo, *Astrology, Psychology & the Four Elements* (Reno, NV: CRCS, 1975), p. 91.

Typology

Psychologically speaking, the four temperaments are the basis of astrological typology. This has been confirmed in modern times by the work of C. G. Jung, who opened up fresh vistas in personal psychology with his four functions. Table 1 shows a useful scheme.

The following are brief descriptions of the four types that include planetary analogies that will help readers gain new perspectives and throw a distinguishing light on the characteristics of the temperaments.

Fire or Intuition Type
(Corresponding to the planetary quality of Mars)

Its properties are active, masculine, dynamic, decisive, able to seize the initiative, positive, freedom-loving, pugnacious, thrusting, ambitious, pushy, individualistic, full of bright ideas, creative, intuitive, fickle, insensitive, choleric.

Earth or Sensation Type
(Corresponding to the planetary quality of Jupiter)

Its properties are objective, practical, economic, purposeful, profiting by advantage, close to nature, alive to the world of

Table 1.   Elements, Planets, Colors and the Jungian Types.

Element	Jungian Type	Planet	Color
Earth	Sensation	Jupiter	Green
Water	Feeling	Venus	Blue
Air	Thinking	Mercury	Yellow
Fire	Intuition	Mars	Red

the senses, epicurean, persevering, tenacious, patient, cautious, lazy, phlegmatic.

Air or Thinking Type
(Corresponding to the planetary quality of Mercury)

Its properties are objectifying, theorizing, studious, clever, intelligent, collating, impartial, critical, analytical-logical, intellectual, culture-conscious, informative, negotiating, communicative, matter-of-fact, adaptable, relativizing, fickle, superficial, sanguine.

Water or Feeling Type
(Corresponding to the planetary quality of Venus)

Its properties are selective, sensitive, subjective, feminine, imaginative, receptive, impressionable, healing, peaceable, harmony-seeking, easy-going, compassionate, devoted, in need of protection, anxious, vulnerable, reserved, temporizing, passive, capricious, melancholy.

Typology and the AP

It is easy to apply the above to Age Progression. When the Age Point passes through the houses, intuition and creativity are activated in each of the fire houses (1, 5, 9), realism and powers of realization in each of the earth houses (2, 6, 10), learning ability and thought in each of the air houses (3, 7, 11), and feeling and a need to belong in each of the water houses (4, 8, 12).

Naturally, the same applies to the AP and the signs in a given horoscope. For example, say the AP passes through the

air sign Gemini in the 8th house (at some time between age 42 and
48 depending on how much of Gemini occupies this house),
then during this period the native will be very interested in
acquiring new knowledge; it meets his or her inner need (sign
= disposition). However, we have to take into consideration
that the environment (fixed 8th house, a water house) con-
fronts him or her with rigid conditions. Psychologically, this
means that emotional ties, obligations, constraints, or lack of
time or money make life difficult. But as the individualistic 9th
and 10th houses are being approached at this stage, the native
will be able to break free for further development, learning,
communication and variety.

I and You Temperaments

A further very instructive distinction is the one between the "I"
and "You" temperaments. This is very significant for psychological interpretation and for the Age Point. The fire and air
signs oppose one another in the zodiac and so do the water and
earth signs; these represent the confrontations between the I
and the You, between the inner and outer worlds. They sym-
bolize the law of polarity of our being, and our striving for
completeness. Fire and air can be regarded as masculine-
active, water and earth as feminine-passive. Air and water, air
and earth, fire and earth, and fire and water do not oppose one
another across the zodiac, but stand side by side in a brotherly-
sisterly relationship. They are mutually supportive. On the
principle "as above, so below," we apply to the houses what has
just been said about the signs. The division is the same.

On the I side of figure 7 (houses 12 and 1), we see water
(Pisces) and Fire (Aries); on the You side (houses 6 and 7), we
have earth (Virgo) and air (Libra). From this we derive the
following classification:

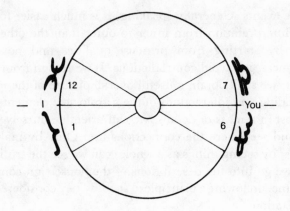

Figure 7.   The I and You temperaments.

Fire and Water are I temperaments.
Earth and Air are You temperaments.

As far as the Age Point is concerned: when our AP is passing
through a fire or water house (1, 4, 5, 8, 9, 12), we can cultivate the I, promote our personality and become self-aware.
This is a good time for realizing our wants and wishes. When
the AP is passing through an earth or air house (2, 3, 6, 7, 10,
11), the time has come to respond to the You and to set aside
our I (our own hopes and desires) or at least to subordinate the
I to the environment.

House/Sign Combination and the Temperaments

Each combination of house and sign is psychological evidence
of the native's problems and development; so let us take a quick
look at some examples, confining our attention to a single
zodiac sign in each case. The reader will note that our conclu-
sions are drawn from first principles, not from symptoms of

concrete events. Generally speaking, it is much easier to work out an interpretation from inner to outer than the other way round. By starting from primary qualities and not from appearances, we avoid contradictions. If we reason from cause to effect, we shall obtain a useful overall picture of the modality, blending and interactions of the astrological elements. Not being lost in a mass of details, we can orientate ourselves correctly and see where the connections are. Only by making a synopsis, by seeing things as a whole, can we see the truth. But before we go into the descriptions of the house/sign combinations, the following principles should be considered for interpretation:

1) It is not often that sign and house coincide. Usually there is a certain amount of overlapping; in which case it is always the sign on the house cusp that counts.

2) When a sign fills the greater part of a house, but the preceding sign is on the cusp, the qualities of the two signs have to be combined.

3) If the sign is intercepted, the sign quality is subordinate to the house theme.

4) Another important factor in making a judgment is whether or not a sign is occupied. Planets represent important psychic forces which must be taken into consideration.

5) In a sign/house combination, we must always bear in mind that signs show what is innate — our disposition — whereas houses show what is expected of us — that is to say, external conditions.

6) Therefore we need to discover whether the qualities of sign and house agree or disagree.

7) In making an interpretation, we should start from the fact that any discrepancy between sign and house indicates developmental tensions that stimulate inner growth. These have an aim, a hidden meaning, that ought to be figured out.

8) The key to this is given by the dynamic counting method.

9) Furthermore, a note can be made of whether we are dealing with a minus house—in which the case the sign is stronger—or with a plus house—in which case the house is stronger. We shall come back to this point in a later chapter.

Fire Houses 1, 5, 9
Combined with
Fire, earth, air, and water signs

Fire/fire:
Aries, Leo, Sagittarius in fire houses 1, 5, 9) Here is agreement. The inner temperament finds confirmation in the world outside, and does not need to adjust to it. However, different qualities of the crosses will produce a complex motivation. Say the *cardinal fire sign Aries is in the mutable 9th house*, then motivation is the field in which there is a transition from the cardinal will cross to the mutable contact cross. As far as the temperaments are concerned, like temperaments can complement or potentize one another. The fire sign is at home with personality development and with the manifestation of the ego in the world. So the ego reigns supreme in both sign and house. In the 1st house, all experiences revolve around self-assertion; in the 5th, they have to do with strengthening the personal influence; in the 9th, they concern the winning and defense of personal freedom.

Earth/Fire:

(Taurus, Virgo, Capricorn in fire houses 1, 5, 9)

Earth and fire have a knife-edge relation-ship. If the fire blazes too fiercely, it is dis-ruptive and scorches the earth. Earth sup-plies fire with materials for burning, and this is mutually beneficial provided everything is kept under con-trol. Growth is brought about by warmth and light. With an earth sign in a fire house there is great practicality. The fire house gives will-power, ambition, courage, and a fund of ideas which earth helps to formulate. The person with this combina-tion will move unerringly toward his or her goal and will not easily be diverted from it. Creative talents and activities make their presence known. If, for instance, the *earth sign Taurus is in the 5th house*, the fire house gives love of action, a readiness to take risks, and the courage to experiment. Safety-first Taurus loses much of its hesitation, but supplies the endurance and stability required for the creative forces to do something con-crete. With the passage of the AP, this house can realize its potential.

Air/Fire:

(Gemini, Libra, Aquarius in fire houses 1, 5, 9)

Since air and fire signs are in opposition, it is possible for them to complement one another. The capacity for thought given by the air signs breezes (so to speak) into the intuitive fire houses. But a very strong wind either extinguishes fire or fans it into an inferno. When the air-flow is moderate, the fire burns quietly and steadily and throws light and heat on the path. In other words, the natural intellect express itself usefully in the environment; yet, at the same time, intuition supplements verbal knowledge, so thinking becomes more comprehensive and universal, and the expansion of consciousness is a goal. For example, if the *air sign Libra is in the 9th house*, the attitude of the native is normally cultivated and philanthropic, and there is a willingness to allow others their rights. However, this fire house (9) will not accept the Libran need of harmony where the integrity of the life or the inner attitude to others is concerned. Real values have to be upheld.

Water/Fire:

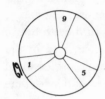

(Cancer, Scorpio, Pisces in fire houses 1, 5, 9)

As energy-types, water and fire are inimical to one another. Fire shrinks from being doused by the element of feeling (water) and water is agitated by fire's threat to disperse it into steam. Nevertheless, processes like these are creative: witness how the sun's rays suck up water and gather it into clouds, ready for the next shower of rain. And the cycle of transformation is at work not only in nature, but also in the horoscope. For instance, if the *water sign Cancer is in the 1st house*, the native's ego will be expressed very emotionally. He or she tends to have subjective reactions and will take many things too personally. Such individuals usually spend themselves for those they love or for those with whom they are closely connected. They do not make selfish demands unless backed into an emotional corner. Passive water signs take a certain amount of rousing. Water/fire transformation alters the ego, and purges it of emotions (such as an exaggerated fear of the environment) — the sort of thing that hinders ego-development.

Earth Houses 2, 6, 10
Combined with
Earth, air, water, and fire signs

Earth/Earth:

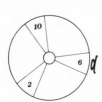

(Taurus, Virgo, Cancer in earth houses 2, 6, 10)

The earth temperament manifests itself fully here. This individual relies on the five senses, on what can be physically observed. He or she sets a premium on common sense and practicality, does not rely on inspiration or theory but on hard facts, and knows how to make the best of his or her abilities. The 2nd house encourages one to conserve energy, and to plan for a big return on a small outlay. In the 6th house every effort is made to safeguard one's existence, and in the 10th house much hard work goes into winning professional advancement. The practical earth element gives patience, perseverance, skill, and stubbornness. Those in whom it is strong try to make sure that no one can get the better of them. Often they cling to order and routine and are interested only in material comfort. Yet even here the basic motives are modified, all according to the crosses involved. If *Taurus is in the mutable 6th house*, the obstinacy of the fixed sign becomes rather more flexible and accommodating. Nevertheless, one must not place too many demands on the native: a Taurean does not take kindly to being exploited.

Air/Earth:

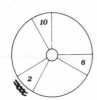

(Gemini, Libra, Aquarius in earth houses 2, 6, 10)

In the earth houses, the air temperament has to adjust to matters of fact, and this give greater depth. Theoretical and high-flown ideas are compelled to prove themselves in practice; something which is often perceived as due to external pressures or constraints, yet gives good results in the long run. For example, if the *air sign Aquarius is in the 2nd house*, ideas and spiritual goals must be turned into deeds. The earth house reduces the soaring thoughts of Aquarius to viable proportions, and this the air temperament finds limiting. The earth-house policy is slow but sure, but Aquarius wants the future now, if only in imagination. Bringing ideas to birth in the material world is the task; making one's vision useful to others the aim.

Water/Earth:

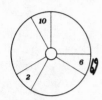

(Cancer, Scorpio, Pisces in earth houses 2, 6, 10)

Water and earth are also polarities, and oppose one another in the horoscope. But they are complementary in the sense that facts are understood and absorbed through the emotions. These elements go well together. Earth acts as a container for water and leads it in fixed channels. This gives water signs the confidence, security, and sense of direction they seek. For instance, if the *water sign Cancer is in the 6th house*, one's feelings for others can be fully released. Maternal functions, such as caring, supervising and nursing, or the desire to be responsible for others, have plenty of scope in the 6th house. If people with this combination find that their concern is not wanted or appreciated, they will creep into their shell and will not come out again without repeated reassurances and expressions of regret from the other party.

Fire/Earth:

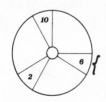

(Aries, Leo, Sagittarius in earth houses 2, 6, 10)

Fire signs in earth houses suggest that inner goals are likely to be achieved. The onrushing fiery energy is molded into concrete realization of the correct form. For example, if *Aries is in the 6th house*, the latter puts an environmental brake on the egocentric impulses of the former, and the native must learn to serve the You, i.e., to serve others, before achieving the eagerly desired recognition.

Air Houses 3, 7, 11
Combined with
Air, water, fire, and earth signs

Air/Air:

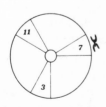

(Gemini, Libra, Aquarius in air houses 3, 7, 11)

When the temperament is repeated its properties are potentized. In this case, the air quality of thinking is stimulated. The native seeks verbal and intellectual exchange, and needs confirmation of his or her opinions, beliefs and doubts. He or she may move in a rarefied atmosphere and lose touch with the direct experience of daily life. Admittedly, this does tend to promote objectivity and discourages fixation on material things, but practical accomplishments are lacking. *Aquarius in the 7th house* can make it easy to get on with people as long as the native keeps them at a distance and deals with them in a general way; but loving care of the current partner is not so much in evidence. In the 3rd house, the views of other individuals or of the group seldom impress, and elicit no more than a brief "I hear you." Someone with Gemini in the 7th house has no respect for the privacy of the other person and is intrusive. Air signs in the 11th house prompt the native to place too high a value on education, intellect and culture, and go with a refusal to admit that the value of ideas has to be proved before they can be treated as dogma.

Water/Air:

(Cancer, Scorpio, Pisces in air houses 3, 7, 11)

In a person with this combination, feeling and understanding either clash or else they stir one another up. The water signs have difficulty in meeting the requirements of the air houses. Personal feelings always enter into the native's attitude. The aloof objectivity of the air houses is quite foreign, and even painful, to sensitive water. For example, if the *water sign Pisces is in the 7th house*, the native will invest a lot of his or her emotions in relationships and will be very devoted. But the 7th house calls for a balanced relationship, a genuine partnership which, either by contract or mutual consent, leaves to each their own. Pisces finds this hard to accept, because it craves emotional commitment and reassurance. Pisces wants to love and be loved: it believes in genuine human ties not legal arrangements.

Fire/Air:

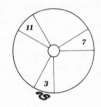

(Aries, Leo, Sagittarius in air houses 3, 7, 11)

Fire and air are poles of a single axis, therefore the two temperaments have a complementary function. Fire burns by means of the oxygen in the air to produce both light and heat. With their intuitive dynamism, the fire signs can react quickly to the mental challenge of the environment. To bring air-house ideas to fruition takes concentrated will-power, and this is just what the fire signs supply. When this combination is dissident, inspiriting energies and creative forces are set free. With *Leo in the 3rd house*, educability depends (from inner necessity) on the quality of the environment. The opinionatedness natural to the fire sign makes for a nonconformity that is often in conflict with orthodox views. If teachers are too dogmatic during the passage of the AP through the 3rd house, the fire sign reacts individualistically and the native becomes obstructive or, in general, shows no interest at all. The central fiery force of Leo must find in the 3rd house's relativizing and equalizing a highmindedness worth accepting. Only then can the lion say a wholehearted Yes, and throw himself heart and soul into the 3rd house, filling it with vitality and living values.

Earth/Air:

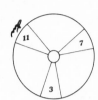

(Taurus, Virgo, Capricorn in air houses 3, 7, 11)
Earth and air can coexist happily. Earth finds it pleasant when the wind blows gently over it (although, when the storm rages, it is disturbed). The practical intelligence of the earth temperament usually meets the requirements of the air houses. For example, if the *earth sign Virgo is in the 11th house*, Virgo will give approval of the ethical standards of friends and others. It will also have a desire to keep the world in order, so that life can proceed smoothly and undisturbed. The slightest disruption of one's vividly imagined hopes and wishes is keenly felt and remembered. With the accumulation of minor disappointments, trust in friends, in the future, and even in life itself can be lost. However, the air house is always ready with new ideals to solace disappointments.

Water Houses 4, 8, 12
Combined with
Water, fire, earth, and air signs

Water/Water:

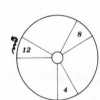

(Cancer, Scorpio, Pisces in water houses 4, 8, 12)
The emotional element flows strongly and steadily here, like a river hurrying to the sea. The natives are largely controlled by emotional impressions. Their evaluation of reality, which is emotionally colored, is derived from their feelings. Today, they are positive and full of optimism; tomorrow, negative, despondent and passive. They react emotionally to all sorts of nuances and subtleties. Others often fail to notice these things, but to them they are very important. In the 4th house they are deeply disappointed if others do not share their per-

ceptions; they feel misunderstood, and are liable to take offense at what they imagine is a personal slight. In the 8th house they passionately desire that others reciprocate their feelings. The 12th house links them with invisible currents from the unconscious or from the universe — often they are kept by protective forces from within themselves, led like small children, guarded and preserved from danger. The element water is closely associated with processes of transformation and purification. This is particularly noticeable when the crosses differ. For example, if the *fixed water sign Scorpio is in the mutable 12th house*, the safety motive dissolves in this uncertain area of universal sharing, breaking down of barriers and transcendence. Inclusiveness comes before safety here. However, those who are unaware of the need for transformation are driven by compulsive ideas and wishes and by irrational fears. The least threat makes them uneasy and defensive.

Fire/Water:

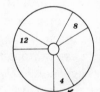

(Aries, Leo, Sagittarius in water houses 4, 8, 12)
Here again we have two hard-to-synthesize elements. In water houses, fire signs will usually raise a lot of steam: the native's goals and wishes conflict with the emotional claims of others. Fire is not accommodating but makes a decidedly egoistic temperament, in which personal interests occupy the foreground. Because of insensitivity, the feelings of others are easily hurt. If, for example, the *fire sign Sagittarius is in the 4th house*, inner freedom, and a clear personal identity will naturally be important; however, the 4th house calls for conformity with the group and serious attention to the duties of family life. Sagittarius instinctively opposes these claims, which are felt to be impositions; so there are problems with the immediate environment. With the passage of the AP through the 4th house, quarrels, misunderstandings and conflicts with relatives must often be endured. It is then that the urge to be free, and the

longing for the wide unfettered world, leads to an early departure from the parental home. Nevertheless, it is through the family friction that the native gradually loses something of his or her "cold individualism" and develops more understanding for others.

Earth/Water:

(Taurus, Virgo, Capricorn in water houses 4, 8, 12)

A natural appreciation of the basic essentials of life, shown by all earth signs, holds the emotional side in check. The earth element bestows on the water element structure and form. Feelings are given an aim, are directed into certain channels, and can be employed constructively. The flowing water element finds a dependable solidity in the earth sign. If, for example, the *earth sign Capricorn is in the 8th house*, the fluid element can be harnessed for use. In practice, this may mean that a secure, preferably top-executive, position is sought that will last until retirement. Of course, as the AP passes through the 8th house, the purifying and purging water element is likely to meet powerful resistance. The native will not give way, holds on to what he or she already has, and refuses to grow further. The Saturnian forces of Capricorn gain the upper hand all too easily, especially when the sign is occupied by planets of the same nature as itself.

Air/Water:

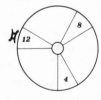

(Gemini, Libra, Aquarius in water houses 4, 8, 12)

Air signs think and talk a great deal, water signs react to the slightest vibration or stirring of air. This combination is always in motion, and responds immediately to everything that is perceived either internally or externally. The thinking principle of the air signs is kept busy by the water houses, but it is not easy to create anything of lasting worth. Thoughts are fleeting and have to be caught and made concrete. The best that can happen in this case is for them to soak into the astral body and fertilize the desire nature; then the natives have an inspiring effect on those around them, and are rather like expectant mothers waiting for the birth of their ideas. Now suppose *Gemini is in the 12th house*; this usually purports an ineffectual struggle for academic honors. The natives are soon irritated, and may even feel threatened, when their opinions are ignored or their intellectual ability is doubted. They believe their ideas deserve serious attention. But there is something they need to learn: their wealth of thought will pay dividends only when cleared through the deep emotions.

The Synthesis of Sign and House

As already mentioned, in working out the meaning of temperament and cross, notice must always be taken of the house concerned and also of the phase of life. A synthesis is derivable only from joint activity. The first thing to do when trying to understand the life situation and problems of an individual at a given age is to define explicitly the basic inner attitude of the sign character (of the cross/temperament combination). This will make it possible to use the basic attitude consciously and positively in tackling external tasks. And here it is worth observing that, even when the environment appears to present hopeless difficulties, the sign quality (our natural talents) can help us solve them.

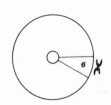

To illustrate what we mean, suppose that Pisces is in the 6th house. Both Pisces and the 6th house belong to the mutable cross; so to this extent they are in agreement. By temperament, however, Pisces is a water sign; but the 6th is an earth house.

This water/earth combination has already been described. Watery Pisces is all for sitting down to watch the world go by. The native will do nothing that is not part of his or her job — unless it is to help someone in need. When others approach, they will be kindly received, and an interest will be taken in their problems; but, after they have gone, the native will do nothing further. It is no good expecting from Pisces the love of activity seen in earth house 6. During the passage of the Age Point through the 6th house, the native is torn between two minds. The 6th house prompts one to get busy, do one's duty, work conscientiously, keep good time, attend to one's everyday affairs, etc.; but with Pisces, none of these promptings will be heeded unless someone else is supervising or begging for help. The activity reflexes are strongest in this and in the 7th house, but reactions are still typically Piscean. How one goes about things depends on the sign quality and on any 6th-house planets. In order to bring the house into harmony with the sign, one has to know and use one's temperament. How then does one go about it?

Let us stay with our example. The quality of Pisces can be used correctly if we learn the "magic of wait-and-see." By keeping quietly yet expectantly active, we develop a certain magnetism which draws to us what we need. But it would be a mistake to sit around without enthusiasm treating the world as boring: opportunities would pass by unnoticed. The synthesis of Pisces and the 6th house is achieved by cultivating inner growth, a readiness to react, a receptive, sensitive response to people and situations. Pisces encourages us to perceive nuances and depths, to react to things going on behind the scenes — to what are seen as the fundamental energies behind appearances.

This is the reason why, even when the AP is passing through Pisces in other houses, we are quite likely to start taking an interest in occult and esoteric matters.

In synthesizing sign and house, we do not oppose the theme of the house, or simply live in accordance with inner need, but endeavor to unite the two—often very disparate—qualities. The secret lies in bringing our inner needs to bear on external problems in a way that will help us to solve the latter more constructively. This is the right approach. The two themes being highlighted by the Age Point in house and sign must always first be seen and understood in combination. As already mentioned, it is the obligation to develop as a human being that is apparent in the confrontation of sign and house. We have devised a numerical method which shows the difference between sign and house as plus and minus scores. Since the method plays a part in refining the psychological interpretation of Age Progression, the following section contains a brief description of how it is used.

Discrepancy Between Signs and Houses

In the dynamic counting method devised by Bruno Huber, the discrepancy between disposition and behavior (sign and house) can be assessed numerically. The individual houses or signs are scored with plus or minus qualities. The values will be found on each computer sheet based on the Huber method. In Table 2 on page 54 the figures are as follows.

On the left in Table 2 are the values of the planets in the three crosses, on the right are the values of the planets in the four temperaments. The upper row of figures gives the values of the planets by sign position (opposite the word Sign), and the middle row gives their values by house position (opposite

Table 2.   Dynamic Counting.

	Crosses: Motivation				Temperaments: Behavior			
	Total	Car.	Fix.	Mut.	Fire	Earth	Air	Water
Sign	96	38	44	14	18	23	20	35
House	104	28	52	24	29	39	14	22
Difference	8	−10	8	+10	11	+16	−6	−13

Virgo 6th house

Cancer 4th house

the word House). The third row shows the difference in value between the sign and house positions.[2]

First we consult a printout to determine the values of the planetary positions in cardinal, fixed or mutable signs/houses and also in fire, earth, air or water signs/houses; plus and minus values being used to offset the signs and houses against one another. If the house values are bigger than the sign values, the result is plus; if smaller, the result is minus. What is more, if the result is plus, the houses and therefore the environment override the disposition; if it is minus, the signs and therefore the disposition dominate the environment. Certain signs, and the houses derived from them, are thrown into prominence when we combine plus and minus quantities in the crosses and temperaments. This happens according to the following rules:

---

[2]Further information on calculation and interpretation will be found in two self-instruction books, *Die dynamische Auszahlmethode: Teil I: Berechnung*, by Michael-A. Huber, and *Entwicklungsprozess im Horoskop: Deutung der dynamischen Auszahlung*, by Louise Huber. At this time, neither of these works is available in English.

1) Plus is combined only with plus, and minus only with minus.

2) Only the highest numbers are combined; those less than 5 can be ignored.

In the above example we combine –10 in the cardinal cross with –13 in the water temperament. This gives us the cardinal water sign, which is Cancer of course. And Cancer corresponds to the 4th house. Thus the 4th house turns out to be a "minus house." Also, on combining +10 in the mutable cross with +16 in the earth temperament, we get the mutable earth sign Virgo, which corresponds to the 6th house; therefore the 6th house is a "plus house."

Generally speaking, most people are strongly influenced by the plus houses, and have learned to function in that area of life. In the minus houses, the signs (i.e., disposition) are stronger. Our milieu has made hardly any impression at all on us, and may have ignored us. We do not have much idea of what goes on in this area of life, have acquired no know-how, and so are either insecure or else uncluttered and free.

The AP Through Plus and Minus Houses

With the passage of the Age Point through the 6th house, which has a high plus value in our example, 6th house problems will be keenly felt between ages 30 and 36. Possibly we shall live in a state of uncertainty, or find ourselves under continual pressure from the circumstances of life with no apparent means of relief. Experiences of this sort will last as long as we resist the demands of the 6th house. A high plus number always indicates an ability to stand stress; and, in the case of the 6th house, it is important to learn to fulfill our daily duties. We ought to accept them gladly, because the process of recognition and acceptance eventually leads to freedom. The very knowledge that a problem and a special task await us in this house offers a solution, because we can consciously come to grips with them.

In Table 2, the 4th house is a minus house and, when the AP passes through it (age 18 through 24), life will probably become rather uncertain. Perhaps the parental home provides little security, and is not a cosy nest. Or perhaps, feeling homeless, we wander around looking for some kindred spirit with whom to form a relationship, though anything permanent seems to be out of the question. Society can be an unknown quantity; often it is a threatening factor—and so is the family. When the Age Point passes through a minus house, we feel rather insecure and helpless; needing know-how, needing to grasp that we have a freedom we can use. By bringing our natural disposition (as represented by the sign) into play, we can become more self-assured.

Interestingly enough, a house with minus numbers offers room to maneuver. To combat a feeling of helplessness, we can take ourselves in hand. Since this area of our life has not been overstructured, we are relatively free to be ourselves; that is to say, we can live in the spirit of the sign occupying the inherited disposition. But this is possible only if we are capable of using our freedom constructively and if, on the strength of what we see and know, we adopt an individual or independent attitude.

As a rule, during the passage of the Age Point through houses with minus values, it is fairly easy to express our natural disposition; whereas during its passage through houses with plus values, a whole pack of habitual reactions or overstructurings must be removed before we can get in touch with our own true will.

More importantly, the study of sign and house brings a conscious realization of the unity of temperament and environment, of inner and outer worlds. The development of this awareness of complex unity is known as individuation. The person who has achieved wholeness by synthesizing the two worlds is free from the horoscope, and is guided entirely by the self and by the real requirements of life, not by imposed standards. In him or her, nature and human nature agree; and it is possible to risk being individual — to the extent of passing one's own moral judgments and taking full responsibility for what one does or does not do.

Having reached this stage, we face the world positively and assimilate it, because we perceive ourselves as part of the whole. We may perform the same tasks as others, but our attitude is different, and usually they recognize it. When we have achieved this inner wholeness and are at one with the universe, our assured personality structure and our expanded awareness make us a tower of strength to many and we become a helper and servant of humankind.

The person who is at loggerheads with the world or who ignorantly refuses life's duties has abandoned the harmonious process of exchange between inner and outer, between above and below. So it is important to seek our center and to remain firmly anchored there; then, in the light of what we now, we can freely decide how to treat the world and its claims.

As long as we repress a part of our being — to which the environment also relates — the horizon is limited and we fail to take advantage of life's possibilities. Our decisions are not well thought out because they do not come from our inner selves; we go by what is customary, or blindly follow the advice of parents or other authority figures who have conditioned us to act according to those standardized forms of behavior which the world calls good or bad, black or white. By escaping from well-entrenched systems, we gain inner freedom, and our ideas of right and wrong become based on conscience and personal knowledge. In other words, our attention is directed more and more to our own center, we become aware of our selfhood and individuality and so recognize the tasks we are meant to accomplish in the world. All this requires a process of continuous self-interrogation and self-control, in which the unconscious is not forgotten. Only when we have discovered for

Figure 8.   The signs of the zodiac on an Egyptian sarcophagus.

ourselves why we ought to do this or that can we assume responsibility for how we live; perhaps doing exactly the same as we did before, but now with a new awareness. There is no further room for the superego, for collective norms, codes, and authorities, or even for the horoscope; the self, as the center of the personality, becomes the arbiter of behavior and approaches the world in a positive and creative manner. This self within, symbolized by the cross in the middle of the horoscope, lives in harmony with cosmic laws — in unity that is with the entire plan of creation. He or she whose life is attuned to the self can do only what serves the Whole. To give an experience of wholeness and to increase human freedom are two of the worthwhile goals of Age Progression.

Chapter Four

The Temperament Age Point:
Four Lines of Development

Since the four temperaments are so closely bound up with the way we do things, a further interesting perspective opens up at any age phase if, beside the normal Age Point, we consider an Age Point traveling through the individual temperament houses.

Following prolonged research and many observations of the various ages and their characteristics, the fact has been confirmed that a combination of the two Age Points is needed for deeper insight into psychological connections. What is more, we may safely say that while the normal Age Point registers the outward behavior noticed by others, the Temperament Age Point reveals our inner development, the maturing processes taking place inside us. The latter is determined by the four temperaments; and it is remarkable that, in practice, the normal Age Point (AP) and the Temperament Age Point (TAP) move synchronously in the horizon houses (the "I" houses 12 and 1, and the "You" houses 6 and 7), move in opposition in the meridian houses representing the confrontation of the group and the individual (axes 4/10 and 3/9), and, finally, move square to one another in the fixed houses (having-being) and thus in strenuous but activating tension. To make matters clearer, we shall begin by giving a table showing the four temperaments and their houses as four different lines of development. See Table 3 on pages 64-65.

Spiral Development

When dealing with the Temperament Age Point, we should note that it does not travel regularly from one house to the next, and yet every now and then, at the cardinal axes AC, IC, DC, MC, it makes an immediate transition to the next temperament house. The resulting spiral line of development runs through the houses as illustrated in Plate 3 on page 99.

Ego development	Fire houses	1	5	9
Social development	Earth houses	10	2	6
Contact development	Air houses	7	11	3
Emotional development	Water houses	4	8	12

In this spiral line of development, the TAP takes eighteen years to move through the three fire houses, and similar periods of time to move through the three earth houses, the three air houses, and the three water houses. This eighteen-year cycle has already been described for the quadrants in *Life Clock Vol. 1*. We shall come back to this later. Incidentally, it is interesting to note that the temperaments were assigned to the quadrants in antiquity. Even the Babylonians saw a correspondence between fire and the 1st quadrant, earth and the 2nd quadrant, air and the 3rd quadrant, and water and the 4th quadrant (see figure 9).

Our study of development will start with the assumption that life can be equated with growth. Each temperament has its

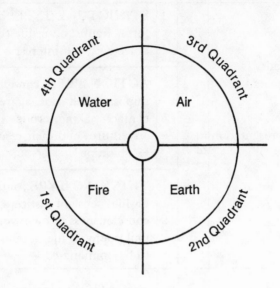

Figure 9. Quadrants and temperaments.

line of development, which begins in a cardinal house, jumps to a fixed house, and ends in a mutable house. The three-stage development process is organic and always leads to greater integration. Those who recognize the pattern try to resolve their problems in a way that allows for growth. Whether or not a situation pleases them, they will forge ahead every now and then and be more or less creative. They tend to be perfectionists, and want to improve themselves and the world; even though they know it is unrealistic to expect a state of perfection of this earth. The urge to make things better is the first step on the road to further development and marks the life of someone with originality, for whom there is no standing still, no resting on their laurels, no holding fast, but a continual advance under the laws of cosmic progress.

Table 3.   Four Lines of Development.

Personality development			
Personality development • Bearing • Self-presentation • Ethics I-extroverted	FIRE 1st quadrant	1	STRUCTURE TYPE: basic form, figure, outer life (image), objectives, self-interest
		5	ACTION TYPE: conduct, imposing behavior, aggressive contact-making, erotic adventures and their results, exploitation
		9	THINKING TYPE: outlook on life, sense of justice, consciousness of own worth, philosophy of life, a tendency to be opinionated
Social development • Authority • Possessions • Performance YOU-introverted	EARTH 2nd quadrant	10	VOCATION: place in the community, self-development, career, aims, authority or presumptiousness
		2	BASIC EQUIPMENT: talents, energy store, advantages, acquisitiveness, one's means, life substance (vitality, finances)
		6	STRUGGLE FOR EXISTENCE: aptitudes, way of working, performance, weaknesses, psychosomatic processes

Table 3. (continued)

External relationships • Ties • Morals • Adaptability YOU-extroverted	A I R 3rd quadrant	7	LEGAL UNIONS: interest in commitment, secure social relationships, contractual relationships, sacrifice of the ego	
		11	CONGENIAL ASSOCIATIONS: freely chosen affiliations, friends, ideals of humanity, the moralist	
		3	NATURAL CONTACTS: neighborly and brotherly — externally given, collective thought-standards	
Inner orientation SELF –understanding –conquest –existence I-introverted	W A T E R 4th quadrant	4	DESCENT: tradition home and hearth, family, group membership	THE SMALL I
		8	DEATH and TRANS-FIGURATION: law of give and take, obligations to the you	THE I IN CRISIS
		12	INTROSPECTION: You-loss, isolation, the non-secular individual	THE BIG I

Personality Development
(Bearing, Self-presentation, Ethics)

As we know, it is from the Ascendant that the Age Point sets out at birth to journey through the house system. In the first six years it transits the 1st house. Now this is the first fire house. Therefore, in the first six years of life, the AP and TAP move side by side. At the age of 6, the AP enters the 2nd house, but the TAP jumps to the next fire house, which is the 5th, and stays there until the native is 12. Between 12 and 18, the normal AP travels through the 3rd house, an air house, while the TAP travels through the facing house 9, in a fire house. During this stage of life, the two Age Points are in opposition. After the first 18 years the fire cycle is finished. The normal AP now moves into the 4th house, while the TAP crosses directly from the 9th house into the 10th, an earth house. The Age Points remain in opposition.

And so, when the native is 18, the normal AP leaves the I-side of the horoscope and enters the YOU-side, and the TAP commences its earth cycle.

The Fire Phase
1st quadrant

The fire temperament is an I-temperament. Therefore all the fire houses (1, 5, 9) have to do with ego-development. The personality starts to develop in the 1st, or Aries, house. In the 5th, or Leo, house it continues to make progress, and in the 9th, or Sagittarius, house it has fully-formed consciousness. Fire begins with the raw ego and ends with the complete individual. There is a time of crisis in the 5th house during which one graduates to personal autonomy. Any planets domiciled in fire houses can be used to promote the development of the native's personality.

If we now bring back into the picture the normal AP, we see that as the latter is moving through the 1st quadrant (ages 0–18) the Temperament Age Point is encouraging ego-development in the three fire signs (1, 5, 9) shown in figure 10. Either way, the unfolding of self-consciousness is the theme. In the 1st house we build our ego-image; in the 5th we are confronted by our own world. We make a deliberate effort to see how far others will let us go, and in encounters with the You we learn a great deal about ourselves. We want to make an impression on others and to show them our best side. Failed friendships and love affairs reveal our weaknesses. Then there is the question of how to treat people. The right way is to be fair and honest, and to act responsibly. When we have learned this, our development shoots into the 9th house. Here there arises a balanced perception of how to use authority and individuality. And the journey continues, as consciousness crosses the MC/IC axis into the 10th house.

Figure 10. Development in the fire temperament.

Social Development
(Authority, Possessions, Performance)

With the earth cycle, social development starts; this, too, lasts for 18 years. Up to age 24 the TAP passes through the 10th house, which is of course an earth house. See figure 11.

As the normal AP moves into the 5th house at 24, the TAP makes a sudden drop into another earth house (2nd house) and remains there for six years. At 30, the normal AP and the TAP both enter the last earth house (6th house). At 36, when the AP and TAP arrive at the DC, the phase of social development is over. After this, the air cycle begins with the entry into the 7th house — and the two Age Points continue to run side by side.

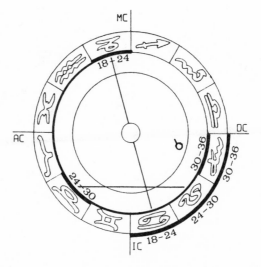

Figure 11.   Development in the earth temperament.

The Earth Phase
2nd quadrant

While the AP is traveling through the earth quadrant (the 2nd at ages 18–36, the TAP is travelling through the earth houses (10, 2, 6). Starting in the 10th house, it continues in the 2nd, and ends in the 6th.

The development of a given temperature always finishes in a mutable house and begins in a cardinal one. Here in the 10th house the interest centers on wielding authority and on becoming proficient in some field. The 2nd house theme is the acquisition of material wealth; and the theme of the 6th house is handing on to others what has been acquired. While developing socially in the earth houses, it is important to prove that one is not an asocial hustler who is simply out for power. True satisfaction arises from benefiting others with the gains gleaned in the 2nd house. This is growth. First comes ambition and planning a career, then the production of wealth, and lastly sharing with the community what one has earned. One must go as an individual to the You in the spirit of helpfulness. This is social progress.

From the 6th house, the TAP crosses over into the cardinal air 7th house. This change to a cardinal house brings resurgent growth, a fresh beginning, new birth. The air temperament deals in externals, so confrontation commences with other human beings, as does a permanent relationship with the environment, with the You.

External Relationships
(Ties, Morals, Adaptability)

Until the 42nd year of life both Age Points are travelling through the 7th house. Then the normal AP carries on through the 8th house while the TAP skips to the 11th.

Subsequently, right up to age 48, the Age Points are square one another. A square does not inevitably mean conflict; it can signal a fruitful learning period where much occurs and progress is made. One longs to exploit one's talents and to do something useful. The final phase of external relationships brings an adaptation to necessities, seeing the TAP is in the 3rd air house; but, at the same time, increased wisdom and a more mature outlook on life, since the normal AP is in the 9th house.

The Air Phase
3rd quadrant

When the normal AP is in the 3rd quadrant (ages 36–54), the TAP is travelling through the air houses (7, 11, 13). The theme of this phase of life is the intelligent understanding and organization of all external contacts. Since this quadrant relates to the

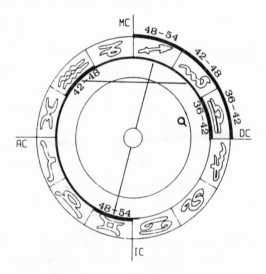

Figure 12. Development in the air temperament.

air temperament, one could hardly expect otherwise. The development spiral begins in the Libra cardinal 7th house, continues in house 11, the individual friendship house, and ends in the collective 3rd house. (See figure 12.) This line of development starts out from abstract intelligence, from pure thought-power. Getting to know the You boosts intelligence. Air always implies contacts, and the thinking we do about these *is* intelligence. At the root of all comprehension lies the contact with object or subject.

The 7th house principle of utilitarian alliances must change if there are ever to be any deep 11th house relationships. At this stage, the realization may dawn that one's motives for getting married were not entirely selfless: personal advantage played a part. We observe the consequences arising from this and start being selective. We look for people possessing spiritual and human worth, not simply material prosperity. Our new contacts must be much more in tune with our inner nature. And so we come to the 11th house and an enhanced and extended knowledge of human beings as such: of their characteristics, their make-up, their ethics. Friendship, in the 11th house, is a solid relationship that is fairly objective. This gain in objectivity brings one to the Gemini 3rd house. The individual feels impelled to transmit his or her universally valid knowledge to the public; perhaps becoming an author, scholar, lecturer or teacher, whose perceptions or learning can then be made widely available.

Inner Orientation
(Self-understanding, Self-conquest, Self-existence)

With the advent of the water cycle, there is a turning from outer life to inner life. Between ages 54 and 60, when the normal AP is traversing the 10th house, the TAP is moving

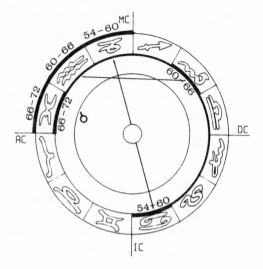

Figure 13. Development in the water temperament.

through the 4th house. At 60, the TAP springs into the 8th house, while the normal AP remains in the quadrant by crossing into the 11th house. Usually this phase of life is beset with difficulties, because detachment from outer things does not come easy. Between ages 36 and 72 the two Age Points meet again in the 12th house. See figure 13.

The Water Phase
4th quadrant

In the 4th quadrant (ages 54–72), the TAP passes through the water houses (4, 8, 12). This is a time of introversion for the purpose of finding oneself and of cultivating inner values—a goal shared by both qualities (by the 4th quadrant and by the water temperature). At 54, the normal AP reaches the MC and the TAP reaches the IC. They are now in exact opposition. We are confronted by ourselves and by all that has already been achieved, as well as by what still needs to be done. We change direction: the normal AP reenters the I-side of the chart and the TAP begins its cycle through the water temperament.

The cardinal 4th house is where the cycle commences. At the outset, we are emotionally embedded in collective life without really giving it much thought. Whether we belong to a sports club, a religious community, a family, or some other group is beside the point; very much to the point is the security provided by an association. What matters is to be with people who think and feel as we do and share the same hopes. The next port of call is the fixed 8th house corresponding to Scorpio. Here we learn that the benefits of safety and security entail obligations. We are required to play our part and to recompense the group or community in some way. There has to be give as well as take. The group's claims are asserted in the name of established custom. It is the group that is found to have rights: the individual has only a limited degree of freedom. Finally comes the 12th house, a water house corresponding to Pisces. Here one seeks a deeper security in the sense of belonging to the cosmos or to nature. Directing one's attention to higher values and goals opens up sources of spiritual strength, brings contentment and a feeling of being back home at last.

Correspondences Between AP and TAP

We shall now endeavor, in a detailed study of the Age Phases and thus of the individual houses, to compare the two Age Points and see how they relate. See figure 14 on page 74. There is this main difference:

1) The normal AP determines outward behavior as seen by the world.

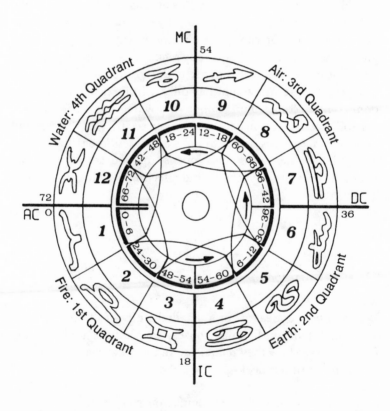

Figure 14.   The developmental spiral.

2) The Temperament Age Point shows inward development, the hidden maturation needed to produce a rounded personality.

Ages 0–6
AP and TAP in the 1st house

From ages 0 to 6,[1] the AP and the TAP go through the 1st house. They keep in step with one another. "Here I am" is the main theme of this manifestation phase of the ego. The fire of ego-manifestation is stoked by the two Age Points so that the I can be cast in its proper form. In infancy concentration on self is very strong. Many children even display autistic traits. Usually a child does not pay close attention to its surroundings until the Low Point (the fourth year of life). All its energies are absorbed by ego-development.

Ages 6–12
AP in the 2nd house, TAP in the 5th house

Between ages 6 and 12, the normal AP is in the 2nd house and the Temperament AP in the 5th, a fire house. The temperament combination is earth and fire. The 2nd house makes the child intensely aware of, and eager to relate to, the environment. It has to win a place for itself and, at the same time, expects to be acknowledged by others. But there are social pressures on the developing ego. The fire theme of the 5th house also comes into play, and it comes into play like this: the child is determined by all means to make an impression. It measures itself against others and wants to excel, wants to have

---

[1]Students should understand that when a child is 6 years old, he has *completed* his sixth year of life, and is now in the seventh. Age 0 may seem odd at first glance, but this is the first year of life.

more than they have, plays all sorts of tricks to get its own way, brags, and shows off its possessions. The child is always testing how far it can go and is constantly pushing at social barriers; and so it experiences a lot about the world and the world's rules, and is continually learning how to get on better with people. At this stage, impressions are formed that govern contacts and behavior later in life, even in the sexual sphere.

Ages 12–18
AP in the 3rd house, TAP in the 9th house

In this phase of life, the two Age Points move in opposition. A tension exists between the desire to learn (3rd house) and the conviction that one already knows everything worth knowing (9th house). There is a wish to preserve one's self-respect when in the company of adults. At this age, many young people would like to have all their questions answered, but their comprehension is limited. Nevertheless, these are the years in which one learns most, not because one thirsts for knowledge, but also because the entire 3/9 thought-axis strongly stresses learning ability. Many youngsters develop grand ideas about life at this period, build castles in the air, construct an imaginary world that usually bears little resemblance to reality but makes them feel good. They cannot stand criticism or reproach, and hate the compulsory instruction represented by the 3rd house. Often they fail at school for this reason. Some of these young people display a practical wisdom beyond their years, and many are true philosophers. But most of them must suffer not being taken seriously, even though their judgment on many issues is usually sound. Their 3rd house AP keeps them tied to their desks, being lectured by teachers.

Ages 18–24
AP in the 4th house, TAP in the 10th house

In this phase of life, the two Age Points are again in opposition. Repeatedly, the adolescent feels that he or she is being pulled this way and that by conflicting tendencies. Young people at the IC often behave as if they were already at the MC. They jib at tutelage and authority and try to claim in advance the power of the 10th house. They want self-determination before they are really ready to look after themselves. In the 4th house most of them are still dependent on their families. All the same, the seed of the individual human being lies hidden here, trying to sprout vigorously via the 4/10 axis. Many parents do not understand these things and feel hurt; they become authoritarian and are met by stubborn resistance. The tension is part of the process of leaving the parental home — normally something which has happened by Low Point four (at the age of 22).

Ages 24–30
AP in the 5th house, TAP in the 2nd house

The fixed houses are always square to one another. This usually means an intense, exhausting period of life that holds in store both duality conflicts and learning processes. Hard tests await us in each fixed house, and we ourselves have prepared them in the preceding cardinal house. Our plans and wishes are now ready to be verified and carried out. The fiery expansive egoism of the 5th house presses outward and seeks to conquer the world. However, the TAP in the 2nd house discourages us from being too pushy. In the 5th house the emphasis is placed, among other things, on erotic and sexual experiences. Sexual activities begin to follow a routine. We discover how well we are able to manage our contacts with others.

Ages 30–36
AP and TAP in the 6th house

Now the two Age Points are travelling side by side once more, and in this way reinforce the quality and demands of the earth 6th house. Social development is forced, and therefore we are kept very busy doing useful work. Besides earning a living, we want to do something meaningful. In the 6th house, the idea is to offer the world what it needs. Success can be ours if we are prepared to help others with their problems. Even when we feel that we are not needed, or even that we are being exploited, it is more important to understand and help others than to cater to self-importance. If we are to make the most of the 6th house, we need to integrate, to make less of ourselves, and to recognize that others have problems too. People at this time of life often change jobs and take up community work: they want to help, to heal, to serve.

Ages 36–42
AP and TAP in the 7th house

Again the two Age Points are moving synchronously, and they stimulate the air temperament and thus the reasoning ability. Now there is a good chance of not repeating our mistakes. We can put into practice what has been learned. No longer so much involved in working and serving, we can make rewarding intellectual and cultural openings for ourselves. In the 7th house we embark upon a process of conscious communication with those around us, because we want to know who is who. Fresh light is thrown on the unconscious, instinctive relationships of earlier periods. The environment becomes a mirror in which we see ourselves and others as we really are. By and large, this is also a period of disillusionment. The 7th house is an "echo chamber," and it sends back to us what we give it. Therefore in confronting the You, whether in marriage or in a business partnership, clarity and honesty of thought are needed. By following this rule, we shall learn a great deal not only about others but also about ourselves.

Ages 42–48
AP in the 8th house, TAP in the 11th house

Now the upper fixed houses are activated. The two Age Points are square one another, and this means that the forces of transformation are armed for conflict. The 8th house holds Scorpio's themes of life and death: things thought to be defunct are now revived. We are confronted by past conditions or habits, and fate lends a hand in testing the humanity and ethics of former pet ideas or avocations, and in probing their fitness for future development. If they meet the demands of the 11th house, they will help us on our way; if they do not meet them, they will become destructive or lead to premature change. Resignation is the result. Thus our inner hopes and wishes (activated by the TAP in the 11th house) encounter the established patterns of the 8th house. For best results, we need to adopt a new mental attitude. This is hard to do in the 8th house, because we are still encumbered by (quite legitimate) matters of social status.

Ages 48–54
AP in the 9th house, TAP in the 3rd house

In this phase the two houses are again in opposition. The 9th house is where our knowledge of life crystallizes into a creed. So, added to the teaching imparted to us by the community in the 3rd house, are the personal experience and independent thought of the 9th. Therefore this period is very suitable for plunging bravely into whatever answers to our inner convictions. In this individualistic house, we ought to become more self-reliant without losing touch with people. Say we developed an inferiority complex in the 3rd house period because we were not as clever as the other children; this is the time to shake free from it—possibly by summoning up the courage to step forward and advocate something we know to be true. Often we come back to those leading ideas of which we dreamed in the 3rd house; now with a real chance of doing something about them. If we are prepared to fight for these ideas, our life will take on a new and deeper meaning that will lead to further progress.

Ages 54–60
AP in the 10th house, TAP in the 4th house

In this period of life, on the vertical individual axis, a mature personality structure is formed which is strong and stable. But the TAP embarks on a water-type development, an inner orientation. This is a paradox. Because of it we are often beset by crises that arise quietly and affect us internally; crises that we do not reveal to others because we do not wish to lose face. Even if we enjoy outward success, and wealth and honor, we may suffer from inner loneliness. We long for the peace and safety, for the cosy nest of the 4th house. Frequently one possesses a certain prestige in the 10th house, and is seen as something of an authority in one's field. It is gratifying to be "somebody," to bask in the recognition of others. On the other hand, we realize our dependence on those who admire us. If they stopped admiring us we should be deprived of the pleasure obtained from their reinforcement of our self-image. Therefore at this time of life there is always a fear of falling from the heights we have scaled. So we must do our best to keep the affection of others, even when we occupy an elevated position. Above has no meaning without below.

Ages 60–66
AP in the 11th house, TAP in the 8th house

The individuation process is resumed here in the 11th house. This presumes, of course, that we now have a wiser head on our shoulders. We have reached a stage when people will expect us to exhibit genuine humanity, culture and morality. The 11th is an air house, and its contacts will challenge our mental and spiritual strength and flexibility. Relationships are fewer but more rewarding. The TAP is in the 8th house of social structure at the very time when we our social position is firmly established but we are no longer in society's pocket. We effect the quiet detachment that comes from inner reorientation (8th house), and step back without being left out. A philosophical attitude needs to be developed that is in touch with reality and accepts that there must be fresh growth everywhere. The person who enters this mature dimension of consciousness will not be lonely, but it is important for the foundations of spiritual development to be laid well in advance if anything is to be solidly and usefully built on them, and if our creativity is still to flourish. As likely as not we shall make friends with individuals to whom we can give something and who are important to us — especially intellectually important; in other words, we shall look for kindred spirits to share our interests.

Ages 66–72
AP and TAP in the 12th house

Once more the two Age Points coincide. In the 12th house we need to be at one with the universe, or to return to source laden with the fruits of experience. There is a tremendous realization of belonging to a cosmic whole; which may be religious in character but also be based on a materialistic concept of the physical universe. We differ as individuals on this point, but the experience is real enough. It is a process that conducts us to the limits of existence and gives either a genuine taste of reality or else a fear of death, before the end. Those who can make peace with themselves and with the world are ready for a new birth and are equipped for a fresh start in life. At the Ascendant there is a renaissance, another beginning, which shuttles us back into the 1st house.

Ages 72–78
AP and TAP in the 1st house

At the 1st house a new cycle begins. The dynamism of the fire temperament imparts a fresh impulse to the remaining years of life. Pep and verve return, and for many senior citizens this is the first time they have really been themselves. In this 1st house, the I-house, one can find out entirely new things about oneself after being given a new inner direction by contact with the boundless space of the 12th house. If one journeys on with the AP, and this is always possible, one starts the cycle all over again, but in a way that is richer and wiser, with fresh standards, fresh outlook, fresh joy of living. Many now stop worrying about the good and bad in life.

Chapter Five

The Age Point
in the Twelve Signs

Having dealt with the significance of the crosses and temperaments, we shall now describe the qualities of each of the zodiac signs as they come into play during the passage of the AP. For the sake of simplicity, we shall ignore the modifications introduced by house, temperament, ruler, planets in sign, planetary aspects, and stage of life. So what we now have to say is by no means comprehensive, and should not be treated as such. Readers may like to work out the modifications for themselves. As already mentioned, the signs consist of a combination of temperament and cross. For example, the mutable air sign is Gemini, the cardinal earth sign is Capricorn. Signs are also categorized according to the Ascendant. Each Ascendant has its own 7th house sign, 11th house sign, and so on. All told there are 12 × 12 = 144 combinations. Within the limits of this book it is impossible to deal with 144 house/sign combinations; nevertheless, we think it will be helpful to the reader to learn the effect of the Age Point in the various zodiac signs and to study the characteristic mental attitudes associated with them.

The AP at "Zero Point"

The zodiac ends in Pisces and begins in Aries. At this juncture the circle is closed; end and beginning, death and rebirth mysteriously meet. We have already written of this in the chapter on the astrological color circle. As the AP ushers you into Aries, you step across the so-called "zero point" of the zodiac where you will probably feel a strange attraction to transcendental matters. Consciously or unconsciously you will be stirred by something that may seem strange and yet familiar. The experience is one of refined energies from subtle spheres reaching you through this "hold." Many individuals are greatly stirred by this, but others are hardly affected; everything depends on openness to spiritual influences. Many are unsettled and do not know what is wrong with them; especially if they are immured in the material world and know nothing of the Self, their true home. Crises involving radical changes may occur in which new life seems to proceed from death. Many feel they have been left defenseless in the grip of some power. Others deliberately await a contact from the spirit world. They open up in prayer, meditation, or religious retreat to subtle, healing forces, or seek a mystical experience of God. Many who have crossed this threshold with the Age Point speak of a "pull," of a longing to return to the home of the soul. The "pull" frequently brings about an inner reversal, a change of motivation, and with it a decisive turning point in life. At all events, a new cycle begins with the entry into Aries, and one ought to prepare for it properly.

AP in Aries

As the AP enters the fire sign Aries, the dynamic fire element springs into action. The "zero point experience" is over, and you prepare for a "rebirth." Now you pluck up the courage to do new things, and are full of vitality and the joy of living. This feeling may prompt you to accept yourself cheerfully for what you are with a sort of youthful unconcern. Even when you are frequently disappointed and do not succeed straight away, you can move hopefully on to new aims. You should not ponder too long, because then you will lose not only the courage but also the power to act and may even become depressed, usually from groundless feelings of guilt. In the Aries period, success lies in quick, decisive action. You will be more of a pioneer, advocating progressive ideas and inspiring others. Aries is an I-sign, so you can also benefit yourself. Quite possibly you must summon up the courage to "look after number one" if you have neglected the needs of your ego during the Pisces period or have sacrificed any of your ideals. Self-development and a sense of identity are now important; your impulses and deeds will be genuinely your own and will not be prompted by others. You are favorably placed to carry out your projects, even against opposition. In everything you do, you may be expected to be yourself and to stick up for yourself, and to be very dynamic, fearless and spontaneous, refusing to be discouraged, and always making independent decisions.

AP in Taurus

When the Age Point is passing through the fixed earth sign Taurus, you need to watch your economic situation. Your existence has to be stabilized, with a realistic approach to aims, plans and tasks. You will be more sparing of your energies than

you were in the previous period, and are likely to be busy
turning to account the ideas and impulses of Aries. Success
comes by working steadily and systematically, and by refusing
to be sidetracked from your purposes and designs. It would be
wise to sustain a regular daily rhythm and to finish whatever
you take in hand. Your life should now become more stable,
with an increase in material, intellectual or emotional wealth.
Whatever you have achieved or obtained can be exploited usefully and economically in life. You should learn to safeguard
what is yours, in case your claims are contested. You accumu-
late, consolidate and utilize, to husband your strength and
make controlled use of what you have. For this you need to be
undisturbed, with time to attend to every detail step by step.
The unfolding of your talents, and the successful deployment of
your material assets, occupy the foreground of your attention.
You can now put something by for a rainy day.

Venus, too, as ruler of this sign, is probably active, especially if in Taurus. You should be able to enjoy the esthetic and
pleasant side of existence, live life to the full, and get ready to
prosper in comfort. Now you can cultivate a well-rounded personality and can grasp what has always been denied you. You
can create a solid base of wealth and goodwill, and earn the
capital to cushion you for many years.

AP in Gemini

When your AP crosses from Taurus into the air sign Gemini,
you immediately feel as if a great burden has been removed,
and you take many things more easily. There is a gain in
flexibility; you are more open, more inquisitive and more ver-
satile. Anything new intrigues you. During this Gemini period
you exhibit greater learning ability and can mend the gaps in
your education. You can learn languages, attend courses and
lectures, or return to school. This is the time to strive for

knowledge and a broader education. You should try to make new friends and acquaintances and should respond positively to the approaches of others. In Gemini you are more accommodating and flexible than you were in Taurus, can adjust more quickly to changed circumstances, and are grateful for variety. Your spontaneity is enliving and makes you adventurous. You are in your element passing on information and knowledge that you yourself have just found useful. By showing what you know, you may win the recognition that has so far eluded you.

The time is ripe for being open to impressions from the environment and to whatever will improve your mind — this includes things that put you in touch with your surroundings, things such as travel, conversation, correspondence and lectures, to name but a few. And your matter-of-fact approach solves emotional problems in human relationships. Truthfulness and objectivity can now be cultivated consciously. Abilities that have lain hidden are ripe for development, and this makes for professional and social success.

AP in Cancer

When you enter with the AP into the emotional sign Cancer, your reactions to your environment are considerably more sensitive than they were in the Gemini period, which promoted intellectual development. You will experience your emotions in a new way. It is no longer easy to hide your feelings; people notice much more quickly what is going on inside you and whether you are happy or not. Now it is opportune to take seriously your longings, and your desire for love and security, and to learn to show them too. You become more capable of giving and accepting love and tenderness. Often, when the AP passes through Cancer, images emerge from the unconscious; childhood memories and parental problems are recollected and call for fresh consideration. Youthful dreams revive, possibly with a chance of being realized at last.

Cancer, the family sign, provides a splendid opportunity for patching up quarrels with relatives, for strengthening the ties of love, for drawing closer to one's kith and kin, and for becoming more firmly rooted in the community, in the family and in one's home ground. At the entry into Cancer, you notice a greater emotional involvement with others and recognize how much a part of your environment you are. The cry for security, for a nest where you feel safe and cosy, is more insistent; but you must avoid isolating yourself and withdrawing sulkily into your crab's shell. Your dear ones should be shown how much they mean to you. There is no longer any point in hiding behind formal behavior, intellectualism or other defense mechanisms. You can openly and honestly tell those you care about that you need them. Most likely you will work to make a "home sweet home," a safe retreat, a protection from harsh reality. If your age is right, you might start a family during Cancer's period.

AP in Leo

Often extra heat is generated by the transition from watery Cancer to fiery Leo. Conformists may become rebels. If, during Cancer's period, you have kow-towed to the opinions of others and have given overmuch credence to them, there is no longer any need to do so. Now you are free to organize your life how you want.

During this period, the structure of your living space is important. It would be good to break away and be your own boss. You can risk doing what you think is right, in accordance with your inner convictions. Other folk's opinions have lost much of their influence with you because you have found the courage to act on your own initiative. With the AP in Leo, you go by what you yourself think and not by the "done thing." Perhaps some of the emotional relationships formed during the Cancer period will irk, because they impede your progress. This may mean that you are on your own again and have to win through independently. For many of us, the lessons to be learned from the experience are to love ourselves a bit more, to adopt a personal stance in society, and to take the views of others at their true value. If you feel that you are the center of your circle, you obtain the full benefit of your innermost powers.

You ought to develop as perfect a picture of yourself as possible, a close-to-life ideal, radiating out from you into the environment and setting an example to others. All according to the house theme or stage of life, you can take the lead mobilizing the energies of others and activating their talents; so that good work is done under your management. You stand out as an individual but, on the other hand, have to take the responsibility for what you do and allow. With your strong personality and increased awareness, you become a support to many and in this way mature from within into a recognized authority.

AP in Virgo

The change from Leo to Virgo is usually very obvious. It may not be particularly comfortable to fall from a ruling into a serving role. You should now confine yourself to whatever is significant for your professional development. You have to forego the distractions and exaggerated ideas of your own importance that arose during the transit of Leo, and must learn to adjust to hard facts. Problems of existence come to the fore in Virgo. Perhaps you need to concentrate on earning a living, to learn new skills or to go on a retraining course. This will involve you in practicalities, technical details or procedural problems, requiring a sense of order, thoroughness, and the paying of strict attention to the matter in hand. It is wise to deal with things systematically, setting sensible targets and keeping them. The emphasis is no longer on the impression you make on others but on your skills and productivity. A social or humanitarian occupation can help to make the most of the qualities of Virgo. You can care for people, put things first for them, and prevent them from making false moves in the first place. With growing confidence, greater fulfillment is possible, thanks to the discernment, selectivity, and analytical gifts of the Virgin, who knows what is good or bad for her. Visits to health farms, dieting, and medical checkups are timely now. Many at this period in their lives (if the house and age allow) enter altruistic callings. They are high-principled and indefatigable, display a social conscience and are happy just to be needed.

AP in Libra

The attitude to partnership changes with the transition from Virgo to Libra. The dependence, not to say submissiveness, of Virgo gives way to freer relationships. Now you can learn more about the You, and take more of a personal interest in people. If you concern yourself with others, you will not stand alone; but you must give something before you can receive anything back. Others come first; you will adapt yourself to them and strive for an equal partnership. For this, tolerance, a readiness to compromise, understanding, tact and diplomacy are required.

As far as possible, you will avoid conflicts and try to bridge the gap between opposing sides. Where there is an impasse, you will make the first move to break it, and will restore peace by resolving problems fairly. You no longer deal in stark black and white, good and bad, either-or, but in subtle qualitative differences. Perceptiveness needs cultivation during the passage through Libra, in order to find true wisdom and harmonious relationships. Probably you will crave love and understanding, and may do all in your power to make yourself agreeable. Your efforts will be devoted increasingly to beauty and harmony, to balance and cultural enjoyment. You are inclined to lean on others and to get by on charm. You tend to avoid unpleasant confrontations and court popularity. This helps to improve your self-image, and you show your partner your better side. But great care is required not to waste time on worthless individuals. You must always seek the right measure, the golden mean between the extremes. Then human relationships will be fulfilling; you will find the right partner and there will be a proper balance between the I and the You.

AP in Scorpio

Scorpio is the sign of transformation, of the processes of change, of death and renewal. Experiences should not be sidestepped now, even when they jeopardize the peace and comfort of the Libra period. You should meet life actively and see where your limits lie. In this period you find that many things alter, because progress never stands still. Nothing lasts forever; everything falls to the scythe of time. Perhaps you will suffer loss or, conversely, gain something for nothing. Many experience the misery of loneliness, yet find in it a challenge to scale spiritual heights. Others are forced to learn wisdom by gazing into the abyss of human nature. After the crisis of change, one should be able to bear up against extremes of sorrow and joy, and should be able to build a solid inner dyke against later floods. Whoever responds to a higher motivation will penetrate deeply into the secrets of life during this period, often overcoming obstacles vigorously if not ruthlessly.

In Scorpio, sexuality can become a problem for many; it ought not to be repressed, but lived positively. In each act of creation, each transformation process, there is a clash of forces. This is nothing to be afraid of, but should be treated as an opportunity to transcend one's limitations. For the most part, the path in this period leads through perpetual destruction and reconstruction and requires constantly renewed effort, and the shedding of anxiety, of outmoded forms of behavior, and of false certainties. What has formerly proved successful may now prove to be useless. Times have altered, and some readjustment is needed. The conquest of fear of the unknown implies a letting go, an abandonment, often an annihilation of the very things to which you used to look for security. But by giving a positive welcome to irrevocable change you will develop new abilities and prepare for the greater freedom offered by Sagittarius.

AP in Sagittarius

The transition to Sagittarius always comes as a respite. Now you can be more mobile and can rise above the limitations life has imposed. You can shake off your fetters, and wholeheartedly espouse some cause you suddenly see is right. You can adopt a positive and affirmative attitude to life and view it in a pleasanter light, feeling it is there to be enjoyed. Now the emphasis is laid on your own autonomous thinking and independence; and you ought to demonstrate that fact. Where there are conflicts you are in a position to lay down the law and to defend the weaker party. You win sympathy as well as influence by your lively interest in the welfare of your fellow-creatures. It is possible for you to transcend your ordinary self, to cast aside the fears of the Scorpio period in order to take a share in life on a larger scale. What is more, you should now indulge your desire for more living space, and undertake journeys, in order to expand your consciousness. You can and should let people see what you know and pass on your experiences of life. You should have clear-cut goals and should think out new ways of achieving them. But you must also be prepared for the isolation that is natural to each individual consciousness. Even when you yourself long fruitlessly for understanding and love, you should not stop sharing with others your insights and your humanity. If you do this, you will be serving higher ends, your life will be meaningful and you will be of use to the greater Whole.

During the Sagittarius period, many are seized by a vague feeling of unrest, which does not allow them to settle down anywhere. The love of freedom, the wanderlust, the irrepressible desire to ferret around, and the constant temptation to set new goals keep them with their luggage packed and ready to go. The time is now ripe to make major journeys. Others discover a new direction in life and are inspired to seek spiritual goals that benefit not only the individual but a higher good. By being ready for action and having the courage of one's convictions, one can bring within reach plans or projects that have been lying on the drawing board for a long time, or have not been attainable until now.

AP in Capricorn

Capricorn is the sign of individuality in which the mature personality takes shape. By this time you should be clear about your personal and occupational goals. You need to take command of your situation in life or assume some kind of leadership. You are unlikely to be deterred by hindrances or failures but, with unflagging strength, doggedness and willingness to work, slowly but surely make your way in the world. You should accept the risk of individuality; or, in other words, should learn to manage your own affairs. The idea now is not to pay too much attention to the opinions of others but to do what you have learned is right.

Capricorn is the sign of the person who stands head and shoulders above the crowd and gets himself or herself noticed. Therefore in the Capricorn period one cannot commit errors without having to pay for them straight away. You need to set to work carefully and not allow yourself to be pressurized or irritated. It is important always to follow a settled pattern, and to develop self-discipline and personal responsibility. Whatever happens you are keen to preserve the quality of your work: not slacking but keeping to the highest standards with perfection in mind. This applies as much to the elaboration of plans as it does to material things.

When you have mastered any area, and have become an authority on it, you are able to insist on concentrating on your aims. People with strong personalities need thick skins; and during the passage of the AP through Capricorn (at any age) they know how to safeguard both themselves and their projects. Their self-belief and sense of mission give them the confidence to tackle the task in hand. They are indomitable, and overcome difficulties with great competence and skill; it is no exaggeration to say that they thrive on difficulties.

AP in Aquarius

In Aquarius, contacts are made with a view to finding true friendship. So-called friends may often have let you down in the past, and now you can give them the cold shoulder without feeling guilty. You have become selective: you recognize your own worth in your association with other men and women. No longer everyone's friend, you learn who will suit you and who will not. Your interest in the happiness of others is not merely intellectual or psychological but represents genuine philanthropy, fairness and warmth. The spirit of fraternity — universal sympathies — can come into their own in Aquarius. The value of everything is correctly judged. Passion, sexual desire, delirious love affairs no longer shake you because you feel neither false emotion nor fanaticism, but can cultivate genuine relationships and strive for spiritual ideals. With this detached attitude, you are in a good position to find others who are on the same wavelength as yourself—others with whom you have a mental affinity. Once you have located your real friends or social unit, you will no longer feel like a stranger on the earth, but will be supported by a bond of loving understanding and shared dreams. Community spirit and teamwork are to be encouraged, as long as there is no sacrifice of individuality within the group.

In these conditions, you will gain in human values, make loyal friends, and will no longer be a slave to the desire for possessions, security and personal advantage. If you concentrate on spirituality and idealism, moral improvement, on the ethics of human equality, the period will be one of great happiness and inner strength, and you will mean much to your friends.

AP in Pisces

In Pisces, the last sign of the zodiac, problems often solve themselves. Things that used to look serious lose their significance. However, with the fishes, one swims out into deep waters for a while. Many feel familiar ground give way beneath their feet when they enter this sign. Their interests may suddenly change. Perhaps they wish to know what lies behind visible appearances. Quite a few dip into religious, occult or esoteric books, start studying the border sciences or astrology, or become aware of subtle influences. Others develop devotion, the spirit of sacrifice and great sensitivity. They feel called to do good and to care for the sick and the poor.

This is the time to show increased concern for others and their needs. You may have to forget your own, often quite minor, complaints in order to relieve major suffering else-where. During this period you should willingly concentrate on your duties and throw yourself wholeheartedly into whatever you do, preferably into social or humanitarian service. In a kindly, sympathetic way, you will see people's good points rather than their bad ones.

It is not possible to be very enterprising at this time, your initiatives come and go so quickly. You must learn to wait patiently for a chance to be more active. But now you can meditate, enter the chambers of the soul, and listen to your inner voice. You will experience the world through an emo-tional sense that conveys subtle experiences to you. Your ego-nature is gradually dissolved: in Pisces the boundaries between the individual and the universe are often obliterated. Due to your deep inner longing for union with the transcendental, you are now prepared to receive guidance, and you summon psy-chic powers from a source within you by mystical introspec-tion, in order to be ready for a fresh start in the next cycle starting at Aries.

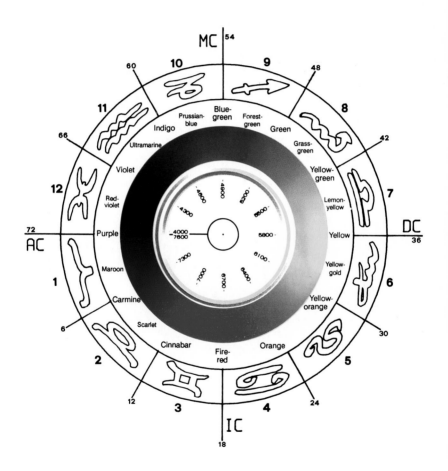

Plate 1. The colors of the natural zodiac.

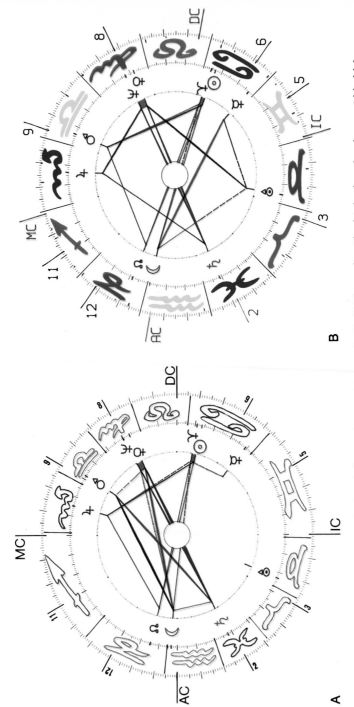

Plate 2. (A) The house chart of a female born July 16, 1935, at 20:45. (B) The radix. The birth place has been withheld for confidentiality.

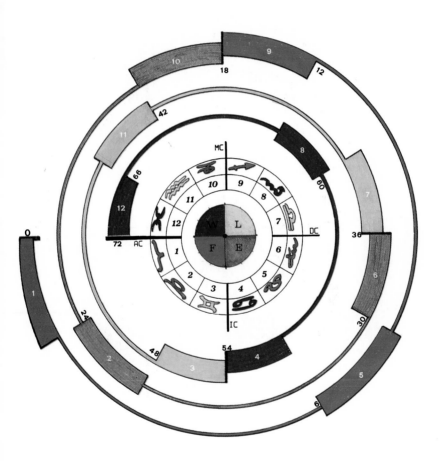

Plate 3. The developmental spiral. Red represents fire, blue is water, yellow is air, and green is earth.

Plate 4. The three crosses. Red is cardinal, blue is fixed, and yellow is mutable.

Part Two

THE SPIRITUAL PATH

Chapter Six

Development
and Evolution

The idea of evolution is an integral part of astrological psychology. The latter is based on a fundamental psychological concept that views a man or woman holistically — as a human being linked both to the immediate environment and to the universe — and as a spiritual entity (individual) who can relate freely and consciously to either.

Taking the idea a stage further, it is postulated that an evolutionary plan runs throughout creation, and that the human soul or spirit has descended into matter from pure, celestial consciousness for the purpose of manifesting in physical form. But the time eventually comes to return to source. The journey back starts with a total inner reversal produced by a sense of the nullity and transience of physical life. Now it is clear, on looking at the spiritual development of individuals, that Age Progression has to do with this journey back. It marks the various stages of evolution in the rhythmic course of life. This law of development is active throughout nature and pro-

Figure 15. Indian zodiac—Jamnapattra of Prince Navanibal Singh.

duces a steady unfolding of the self, as it germinates, ripens and dies.

A knowledge of this evolutionary theory gives us a better sense of time. By looking down a longer vista, we expand our consciousness and improve our understanding of the present. We gain a general view of our own life and of the evolutionary history of our race, and penetrate to the meaning behind everything. This developmental dynamics underlies all that happens to us and its aim is to make us complete and to correct any faults of personality we may have acquired. By making us complete, we mean to help each of us to become whole, undivided beings. From this standpoint, everything we experience as shown in the horoscope makes sense; everything has a symbolic meaning for our further development. That is the fundamental idea of astrological development theory.

We shall now endeavor to elucidate the above from various points of view, while also looking at the parallel idea of Age Progression as a dynamic element of development for the personality. Since our personal lives are embedded in a greater cosmic event, it will be wise to proceed from above to below, from bigger to smaller, in studying these patterns. We must first see the laws of development at work in a wider setting before we can understand their possible effects on our relatively insignificant human lives.

Microcosm and Macrocosm

As we all know, man/woman is the "microcosm in the macrocosm," a little copy of larger cosmic realities. Each of us is only a part — a minute part — of an immeasurable and all-embracing whole, the cosmic whole. The living energies penetrating ourselves and nature are the energies of a great Life, in which we live and move and have our being.

The relating of small to big, of humanity to the universe, and the consideration of all human problems from the standpoint of the one Life, gives a proper sense of proportion and direction, correct evaluation and judgment, and a deeper understanding of the connectedness of things.

The development changes taking place in nature and in human beings are always in the direction of balance and maturity. We can observe this everywhere: in biology, in the life of animals, in sociology, in human relationships; also in the universe, in the histories of the planets and the fixed stars, and even in the galaxies. Everything is governed by a wonderful order that keeps it in balance. Whenever the balance is disturbed, nature finds ways and means of restoring it. Often the remedy is surprisingly drastic, for reasons that are hard for us to understand.

Eastern Theories of Development
(Karma and Reincarnation)

The Hindu and Buddhist religions offer reincarnation and karmic law as an explanation of the balancing process. They assume that the life within us is imperishable, and that only the form or body is subject to physical laws and to death; while the spirit, soul, or self endures—repeatedly incarnating on earth according to the laws of evolution in order to acquire a complete experience of the universe. Their teaching is that each individual has been set an evolutionary goal impossible to reach in a single life. Therefore numerous opportunities are given of getting closer to this goal in different lives. The rebirth or reincarnation from Oriental religion involves a cyclic development that continues until the individual has reached the desired state of perfection and can manifest on earth as a fully functional child of the Deity.

The questions "Where do I come from?" "Why was I born?" "What is the purpose of my life?" "Why must I suffer like this?" "Why are the lives of others so much easier than mine?" are explained by the law of karma. This is the law of cause and effect, which invariably strives for balanced development. Nothing can be thought, wished or done by a person without being lodged in the great energy store of the cosmos ready to come home to roost one day. Hence different destinies—one person possesses everything he or she needs, while another is fighting for physical survival.

According to eastern philosophy, the law of karma plays a double role: firstly, the individual is forced to pay debts accumulated in former lives; and, secondly, he or she develops further under the law of cause and effect and learns not to do certain things because of their unfortunate results. It is intelligence, discrimination, and decisiveness that are liberating here.

This fits in well with what we have gleaned from psychological astrology. People are compelled by the rough-and-tumble of life to develop abilities, many of which have been slumbering all unknown in the unconscious. We learn from experience to bring about an increasingly positive exchange between our inner being and the environment. By rousing our innermost nature to consciousness, we can release ourselves more and more from coercion by our stars, acting as these do through unconscious drives, faulty mental attitudes, groundless fears and paranoia, guilt feelings and delusions—or, in other words, through our karma.

But, when all is said and done, it does not matter what names we give to these active forces, provided we understand them and deal with them correctly. The very knowledge that problems arise from inherited factors, from transferring to the environment our connection with father and mother—or the knowledge that the causes of difficulties lie in karma—helps us to rid ourselves of these problems and difficulties or, at least, to

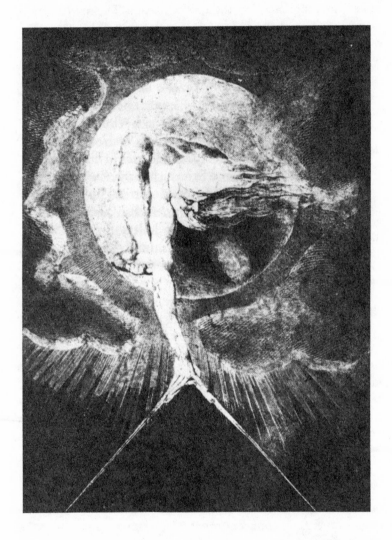

Figure 16. *The Ancient of Days*, a vision of creation by the mystical artist and poet, William Blake.

adopt a different attitude towards them. What matters is to recognize the causal relations affecting us.

Causality: The Law of Cause and Effect "Karma" in Age Progression

Age progression as a cyclic phenomenon has much to do with the law of cause and effect. "We reap what we sow." The AP enables us to see at a glance the native's whole life — past, present and future. It enables us to pinpoint the period in which a given error is committed, or some decision is made that later results in favorable or unfavorable circumstances.

We recognize what made us react in a certain way; whether, at the time, we did so consciously or unconsciously. As already mentioned, it does not matter if we view our impulses as due to predetermination, compulsion mechanisms, or karma. In any case, it seems that karmic law operates essentially in the unconscious. Our blind reactions arise chiefly out of our instinctual nature — the three basic drives: self-preservation (hunger, thirst), reproduction (sexuality) and self-assertion. The law of cause and effect is decisive in the realm of the drives and instincts. When we are functioning in this area, we are ruled by our drives. It is this response mechanism, which is automatically for or against a thing, that is always creating fresh karma in reprisal.

If, for example, someone sticks out a leg and trips us, we get angry and aggressive. Our automatic reaction is to pay him back in kind. Great self-control is required to behave as if nothing had happened; but, if we immediately and blindly give way to a desire for revenge, we shall remain subject to the law of karma. Our action will come back to us like a boomerang. If, on the other hand, we succeed in not reacting or even in taking into consideration the motives of the person who tripped us, then we come to grips with the causes and help to efface the karma. Individual development aims at positive control both of oneself and of one's surroundings, and at freedom from compulsions and contingencies, from inner needs and desires. Here is where modern psychological and spiritual insights prove useful. They permit us to take stock of ourselves, to recognize both our potential and our limitations. Astrology gives similar assistance.

Thanks to Age Progression, astrological psychology allows continual self-observation, self-knowledge, and self-mastery. Finally, an understanding of the mechanisms underlying the way we function permits us to recognize trends in our mental and spiritual development, and also possible dangers and karmic repercussions.

In a horoscope, there are many factors that can indicate circumstances that are more or less forced on the native. We shall not enumerate them all here. However, the karmic components of the three crosses do deserve scrutiny, because the qualities of the crosses point to deep layers of human motivation. In the following section we shall take a closer look at these.

The Course of Life in the Crosses
(Cardinal, Fixed, Mutable)

In considering the Age Point, we need to remember that more often than not the matters indicated related to our environment and not to ourselves. They will thrust themselves on us unrelentingly until we have sorted them out. If we fail to do so while the AP is in the house where they first arise, they will return to haunt us afterward and will then be harder to remedy. Everything left undone must be tackled later with more effort and possibly less success.

For example, problems that were not solved in the 5th house recur in the 8th house, but in a more severe, acute and troublesome form. There are certain sets of problems that are strung together by the same cross. That is to say, similar problems or situations keep cropping up in the same cross as the corresponding stage of life is reached. If, owing to anxieties or taboos, we fail to experience true love in the fixed 5th house, the problem will arise again more sharply in the fixed 8th house. Frequently, our whole way of life and place in society are put at risk. Then if, in the 8th house, we do not come to terms with inner change, we shall have no chance of possessing true friends in the 11th house. It is instructive to look at this topic in relation to the axes.

Karmic Problems in the Axes[1]

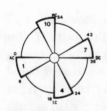

In the cardinal cross, karmic problems arise from the I-You relationship of the encounter-axis (houses 1 and 7). In the 1st house, especially in the first 4 years, the infant experiences self-preservation and self-assertion drives only. This is the time of ego-formation. Others do not yet consciously exist for the child. If, through external circumstances, lack of affection, or breaking of the will, the ego is thrown back on itself, it hardens and becomes incapable of love. The ease with which we make contacts largely depends on the first years of life. If they are unhappy, we shall have to cope with partnership problems at ages 36–42, when the Age Point is traversing the 7th house. What is more, our I-problem or egocentricity will be

---

[1]See also page 143 in *Astrological Houses: A Psychological View of Man and His World* (York Beach, ME: Samuel Weiser, 1984) for more information.

activated when the Age Point passes through the 4th house between ages 18 and 24. Misguided behavior in contacts and intimate relationships will bring painful experiences. We shall lack understanding and love from partner and friends until we learn to give love. In the 7th house we shall be involved in continual confrontation, struggle and strife with the You, until we achieve a harmonious balance between them and us. Whatever we have done to them has to be made good. Divorce is common at this stage of life.

In the other cardinal axis (houses 4 and 10), we usually reap in the 10th house, from ages 54 to 60, what we have sown in the 4th (and also in the 7th) house. If we have treated others fairly and squarely and have scrupulously discharged obligations and responsibilities, then we shall be accorded honor and recognition in the 10th house. But if we have refused to make terms with those who have something against us, or if we have gained a position by unjust means, then karma will catch up with us at this stage. We shall be hurled from our throne, firmly put in our place, or cold-shouldered.

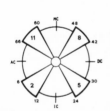

In the fixed cross karma shows up in all fixed requirements or conditions. If, for example, when the Age Point was passing through the 2nd house (between ages 6 and 12), we felt unduly pressurized by those around us and built a defense system against them, we may be disappointed in love in the 5th house (between ages 24 and 30), because we make it too hard for the You to get to us. If this problem is unsolved, or if our attitude hardens still further, the process of change taking place when the Age Point traverses the 8th house (between ages 42 and 48) will be intensified. The dying and becoming, the letting go of material security, the conquest of problems stemming from wrong behavior in the periods of the 2nd and 5th houses require greater effort. Fate cracks down hard, especially at the Low Point of the 8th house (ages 45–46), or when the house cusp is crossed, or upon entry into the sign occupying the 8th house. Many of us then need to take a few blows to shake us out of our set ways and to breach the walls we have built around ourselves in a wrongly conceived scheme of self-defense.

The other fixed-cross axis (houses 5 and 11) also has to do with the development of fixed patterns of behavior. If, in the 5th house (between ages 24 and 30), we fight shy of love affairs because we fear bad experiences or because of moral inhibitions, we cannot experience the 5th house as it really is. Usually in the 8th house (ages 42–48) and even in the 11th house (ages 60–66), we get further opportunities to discover what we have missed. We may start flirting like teenagers! However, the lost opportunities will return only when true love is awakened as an energetic inner power. For, in the 8th house, where rigidity sets in all too easily and there is a danger that existence will become mere routine, love is a healing, life-giving element. But make-shift experiences, in which we merely buy love or friendship, will quickly disappear; leaving behind a bitter emptiness, which can lead to resignation or to a mental crisis in which life seems futile.

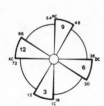

In the mutable cross karma involves questions of both material and spiritual existence. During the passage through the 9th house (ages 48–54), impressions from the 3rd house (ages 12–18) have a marked effect. Even if, at the earlier age, we allowed ourselves to be worsted by the environment, agreed to toe the party line and lost our ideals in time-serving, there is still a possibility in the 9th house of developing individuality and finding our own life-style; especially if our personal conceptions of the world, and our dreams, visions, and youthful ideals, remain alive in us.

The other cross (houses 6 and 12) supplies a direct karmic relationship, too, for what we have achieved in the 6th house (ages 30–36) in terms of civic responsibility, sharing in the community, acceptance of obligations and involvement in social service will contribute to our inner peace in the 12th house (ages 66–72).

If we have served others and have been neighborly, then assistance and further instruction can mean something to us in the 9th house, for in the 6th house we have prepared ourselves for them and can "come home" with a clear conscience in the 12th house. But if in the 6th house (ages 30–36) we shirked work, did not labor for our bread and lived at the expense of others, we cannot progress in the 9th house (ages 48–54). If we possess material wealth without ever having had to struggle for it, the question will arise in the 9th house and especially at the crisis of meaning at the Low Point (ages 51–52): "What can possibly require my attention? I have all I want for myself—what more should I do?" We stagnate, our souls wither, and we find no entry to the spiritual home in old age. Its door has been bolted by our own hands.

Chapter Seven

The Age Point
in the Nodal Chart

We come now to a new line of research into human destiny, namely the lunar node system. Since this is an advanced and highly important element in interpretation, both for spiritual development and for modern therapeutic practice, it may be helpful to give a brief description of the astronomical data.

The moon revolves round our earth in the same way as the earth revolves round the sun. The two orbits, when superimposed, cut one another at points we can calculate. These points of intersection are the lunar nodes. The point where the moon crosses the ecliptic to move out of the southern half into the northern half of its orbit is the ascending node. Exactly opposite this is the descending node. The imaginary line joining the two points is known as the line of nodes, and is important for predicting eclipses of the sun and moon. See figure 17 on page 116.

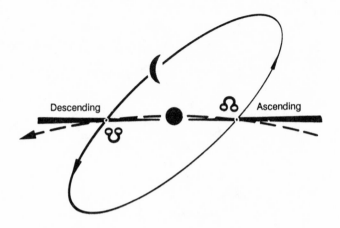

Figure 17. The lunar nodes.

The Lunar Houses

Just as we divide the sun's apparent path into twelve zodiac signs, so — taking the ascending node as our starting point — we can divide the moon's path into twelve lunar houses. Technically, this is quite simple: commencing at the ascending node, thirty degrees are counted in a **clockwise** direction. (See figure 18.) This brings us to the cusp of the 2nd lunar house; another thirty degrees brings us to the cusp of the 3rd lunar house, and so on.

Another method is to place the transparent plastic API aspect finder over the birth chart and to superimpose the aspect finder's ascending node (= AC) on the radical node. Then the twelve lunar houses can be read clockwise to give the so-called lunar node horoscope, in which the radical planets usually have

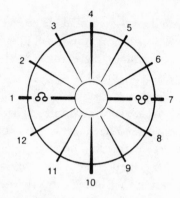

Figure 18. Determining the lunar houses.

new house positions. Simpler still is the use of the API Computer Cortex.[1]

The Shadow Function of the Nodal Chart

In essence, the nodal chart has to do with our desire nature, all the controlled and uncontrolled psychic factors from the past that are stored in the lunar node system. Looked at esoterically, it symbolizes our astral body. It is the so-called mirror sphere, where our motivations, wishes and deeds are projected from the past (our karma) into the present.

In terms of depth psychology, the lunar node horoscope makes the shadow of our personality visible. We all have an invisible part of our being containing drives, wishes and pro-

---

[1]For more information about the plastic API aspect finder and the API Computer Cortex, write to the authors at Astrologische-Psychologisches Institute, Obertilistrasse 4, Postfach, CH-8134 Adliswil, Zurich, Switzerland; or write to the English Huber School, PO Box 9, Totnes, Devon TQ9 5YN, England.

jections. The latter are not amenable to everyday consciousness, and we tend to suppress them as being unusable in ordinary life or even potentially dangerous. So the shadow is often
regarded as negative or "black."

Of course, there are also positive factors which indicate
good karma. There are, for example, spiritual longings that
may be totally suppressed because they do not fit in with some
mental dogma or because they do not happen to be fashion-
able. But even if we ignore them they are still a part of us.
Modern reincarnation therapy is concerned with such factors;
by reliving past experiences, these factors are made conscious
and reveal causes that can exploit the apparently acausal.

C. G. Jung speaks of the shadow; a rather inaccessible
part of the unconscious, which today is explored only in depth
psychology. The human conscious and unconscious resemble
an iceberg with no more than the tip projecting above the
surface of the sea. The visible part is the conscious, the invisible part is the unconscious and in this we find the shadow
personality. We are hardly aware of the motivations, secret
wishes, or splinters of the ego hiding in this shadow region;
often we cannot even envisage, let alone admit them. At most,
they appear in our dreams. Nevertheless, they do exert an
influence on our lives; but usually we fail to associate them
with ourselves, because they manifest as results of our unconscious projections. They appear right out of the blue, in the
guise of situations, issues, or people entering our lives from
outside. They seem to attract to us with magnetic force the very
things we dread and repress. Many an external situation is
misleading because, like a mirage, it is only a reflection. We
cannot handle it properly while we see it as "out there" and not
belonging to us. All too often, the consequences of this shadow
function remain beyond our control. They seem to be forced
on us or to be things we do automatically. Generally speaking,
they have to be experienced negatively before we are able to
connect them with ourselves. However, in the lunar node (LN)

chart using modern techniques of interpretation, we can achieve a conscious understanding of our "shadow."[2]

The Lunar Node Age Point

The lunar node system has a time dimension and Age Progression of its own. We allow the same period of time (72 years) for the Lunar Node Age Point to move round the chart, as we do for the radical Age Point. The Lunar Node Age Point sets out from the ascending node and travels *clockwise* (i.e., in the opposite direction of the normal Age Point) through one house after another, spending six years in each.

Since the lunar houses are a uniform thirty degrees, five degrees always equals one year of life. The years corresponding to a given number of degrees can be read directly from the LN Age Point sheet of the API Computer Cortex or from the aspect finder. Thus we can immediately see where we are in the lunar house system at the age of 45. (See figure 19 on page 120). As the Lunar Node Age Point travels along, the previously mentioned qualities of the shadow can enter consciousness in many shapes and forms, and can produce behavior for which it is difficult to give a reason. Also they can stir up powerful emotions, compensatory actions, and regression to earlier forms of behavior, in which we keep repeating the same old reactions. With regard to the Lunar Node Age Point, it is quite possible to see as karmic components things which, in reality, are nothing more than psychic automatisms. They come from the deepest layers of the unconscious, from the repressed or unlived shadow region of our psyche; and, when the LN Age Point transits a planet, they can look like the workings of fate or karma.

---

[2]See also *Mondknoten-Horoskop*, by Bruno and Louise Huber, published by Astrologisch-Psychologisches Institut, Adliswil, Zurich, 1990. This work is not currently available in English.

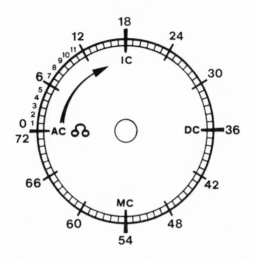

Figure 19. The Age Point of the nodal chart travels clockwise.

Perhaps an example will make this clearer. A lady had Venus on the cusp of the 9th radical house. At a certain stage in her life, she lost her entire fortune. She could not understand why and blamed her husband. Further calculation placed Venus on the cusp of the 2nd lunar house, which suggested that in the past and especially, perhaps, in some past life, there was an accumulation of material goods and wealth (Venus on the 2nd cusp) that was balanced in the present life by the loss of everything (Venus on the 8th cusp).

However, the interpretation is not always so simple and straight-forward. Our example is something of an exception in this respect. The reader is urged to write down the fateful events in his or her life. Often the LN Age Point has no perceptible effect; but often there is a vague stimulation due to planets activated by the LN Age Point.

Comparisons of the Radix AP with the LN-AP

Interesting facts emerge when the two Age Points are compared. In the case of spiritual development, the Lunar Node Age Point frequently plays a bigger part than the radical AP does. At the end of this chapter we will discuss the horoscope of an important spiritual teacher, Jiddu Krishnamurti, for whom the Lunar Node AP brought essentially spiritual breakthroughs. It is fascinating to observe the joint action of the two Age Points. With the radical Age Point, we are looking at the rational side of the psyche and at comprehensible processes that either produce events or are evoked by events. On examining the lunar chart, we come face to face with subliminal motives, the real reasons why we did or are doing this or that. Here we are digging down to a deeper layer of motivation capable of explaining a great deal that was formerly inexplicable. Now, if we are sufficiently strong-minded and our powers of intelligent discernment are in good working order, we can start rooting out some of the things responsible for our faulty attitudes.

Encounter of the Two Age Points

In this lunar node system, there are two points at which, twice in a life-time, the AP of the normal house system (moving counterclockwise) meets the AP of the lunar node house system (moving clockwise). See figure 20 on page 122.

These encounter points can be pivotal in our experience. Maybe we do not know this at the time, but it usually becomes obvious when we look back. In general, the changes involved take place slowly and sneakily. They can commence two or three years before the encounter but may not be noticed until two to five years afterward. The two encounter points lie on a house axis and are defined by the theme of the house and the

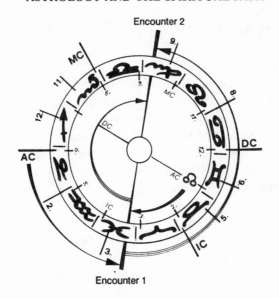

Figure 20.   The encounter of two Age Points.

axis. When, for example, the "encounter axis" is on the 1/7 plane from the AC to the DC, there will be an I-You problem sometime in the native's life. If the two encounter points are on the 2/8 axis, possessions will pose problems; if they are on the 3/9 axis, the problems will be intellectual.

The first meeting between the Age Points happens between birth and the thirty-sixth year of life; the second between the thirty-sixth and the seventy-second year of life. Exactly thirty-six years separate the two encounters. The timing of the encounters is different for each of us, because it depends on the positions of the nodes in the individual chart. If the encounter points lie on the 3/9 axis, the first meeting will occur in the 3rd house (about age 14), and the second will occur in the opposite house (around age 50). These encounter axes must not be confounded with the line of nodes however.

In general, it is true to say that if the life has been rather passive prior to the first encounter and we have been led and molded by others, then afterward we become more dominant and tend to go on the offensive in life; whereas, if previously we have been more extroverted, afterward we become more quiet, more passive, more defensive. The first encounter of the two Age Points is usually quite striking. If our subsequent development is considerable, the second encounter may almost escape notice. Should the effects of the second encounter be strong and drastic, this shows how little we have learned in the intervening thirty-six years.

There is also a good chance of sharp, incisive events occurring at the encounter points; events such as ruptures and bolts from the blue that alter the very nature of our existence. For instance, sometimes those by whom we have been dominated and restricted simply pack up and go, leaving us free to live our own lives. Many will say, "I have paid off my karma and can do what I really want to do at last."

Everyone is more or less exposed to sudden twists of fate which defy rational explanation yet completely change our lives. More than one astrologer has vainly looked to traditional prognostic techniques for some clue to the mystery; but often the only astrological solution is to be found in an encounter of the two Age Points. Anyone baffled by some experience would do well to consider the possible effect of one or other of the encounter points.

The Horoscope of Jiddu Krishnamurti
A Contribution by Marianne Glunz

Krishnamurti (see figure 21 on page 124) has a very special place among the numerous Indian gurus who have imparted spiritual knowledge to the West in this century. He spoke of an "uncharted land of truth," to be found neither by a special path nor by chelaship, but only through the most unflinching self-

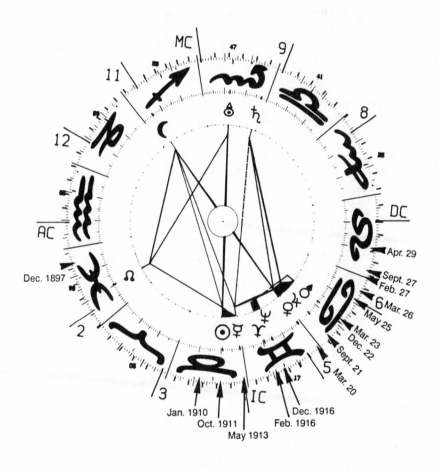

Figure 21.   Jiddu Krishnamurti, born May 12, 1895, 00h30, Madanapalle, India. Chart includes Age Point dates.

observation, as the only thing that can bring freedom from the I and lead to full union with the truth.

When a youth, Krishnamurti was named by the Theosophical Society in Southern India as the vessel for the expected appearance of the highest master, and was given an appropriately rigorous upbringing. After years of internal struggle and in an unparalleled act of repudiation, he rejected this idea and dissolved "The Order of the Star in the East" founded in his honor. Subsequently, to all who were willing to hear him, he spoke merely as a spiritual philosopher with no disciples and no organization.

Krishnamurti's chart is strikingly vertical in its planetary arrangement. The Sun-Uranus opposition is practically perpendicular; and so is the quincunx, the long green "ideas" aspect occupying the thought axis between the two planets of intelligence, Mercury and Saturn. Only slightly tilted, in the 11th and 9th houses respectively, we have the Moon-Venus opposition and trines of Saturn to Venus and Jupiter. So there are clear indications of a striving toward spirituality and toward becoming conscious as an individual. The center of gravity of this striving lies in the 9th house, the upper pole of the thought axis, with Uranus at the Low Point and Saturn near the cusp, both in the dying and becoming sign of Scorpio. Thus an inescapable link is forged between the opposition and the quincunx. Original thought (9th house) and the transmission of ideas (3rd house) are the main themes of this life. While Uranus makes an ambivalent configuration with the Sun and the lunar nodes, Saturn "stokes up" a prolonged conjunction of Venus and Jupiter with a minor influence from Mars. Venus, on her part, is the pivot of the tense Venus-Moon-Mercury configuration, which makes contact with the ambivalent configuration via a weak conjunction of Mercury and the Sun. Potentially, there is great spiritual power through the conjunction of Neptune and Pluto in Gemini, which, scarcely affected by the other forces of the psyche, leads a life of its own in the soul's depths.

The obvious supporting pillar of Krishnamurti's being is
the Sun-Uranus opposition and the Saturn-Mercury quincunx along the thought axis. Uranus carries great weight not
only from its position at the top of the chart, but from its
rulership of Aquarius, the rising sign. Krishnamurti's revolutionary spirituality, his unrelenting calling-in-question of ide-
ologies and religious dogmas, derives from this opposition
and this quincunx: on the one hand there is his early education in Theosophical theory, represented by the 3rd house,
and on the other hand there is his 9th house abandonment of
the inculcated forms of thought, his abrupt rejection of all
assertions on spiritual matters that do not come from innate
cognition. He overstepped normal limits not only geographi-
cally (he travelled widely), but also in two great changes of
life-style: first, through his contact with the Theosophists, he
left behind his familiar traditional Hindu milieu, and then he
broke free from Theosophical circles in order to go his own
way. By so doing he fulfilled an inner urge, indicated by the
lunar node. As it happens, the latter showed a possible way
out of the opposition via the blue aspects: he could rely on
considerable private resources given by the closeness of the
node to the 2nd cusp. Because Pisces is on the cusp, these
resources were spiritual rather than material, and he was able
to share with others the personal knowledge springing from
the fullness of his inner being.

The person who initiated Krishnamurti at the beginning
of his spiritual journey was Annie Besant, president of the
Theosophical Society, who was surrogate mother (he lost his
mother when he was young) and spiritual guide rolled into
one. Saturn in the 9th house marvellously expresses the two
things, and its placement mirrors his relationship with this
woman. The love and esteem with which he repaid her (Saturn trine Venus and Jupiter) were undiminished by Krishnamurti's rejection of Theosophy.

In addition to its relevance at this personal level, the Saturn-Jupiter trine was particularly important in his spiritual development. With Saturn in the 9th house in Scorpio, we have pronounced philosophical leanings: a looking for basic truths and a searching inquiry (Saturn) into the meaning of life (Jupiter). Interestingly enough, the same aspect appears in the charts of Kepler, C. G. Jung, and Heidegger.

At the entrance to Krishnamurti's path stood the image of the spiritual guru: the highest master, whose vessel he was said to be. However, through mental and physical dying and becoming processes (Saturn) Krishnamurti attained a highest knowledge that invalidated, for him, the highest master role. With a Scorpionic hatred of compromise, he then refused all master-and-pupil relationships, all devotees and followers.

The second, upward-striving opposition, between Venus and the Moon along the relationship axis, reveals a certain difficulty in his approach to contacts. Owing to his tactful, sensible behavior he soon became universally loved, which is not surprising with the Venus-Jupiter conjunction in the 5th house; yet from time to time he suffered from great loneliness and could hardly bear to have anyone near him while his fiercest inner struggles were going on. The 11th house cusp placement of the Moon denied full enjoyment of the social popularity promised by the 5th house. More and more he became a teacher of the present generation: endeavoring to instruct the general public (3rd, 4th and 5th houses) from the insights he had gained (11th house). Among other things, he displayed a great interest in the question of education (Jupiter, 5th house, Cancer) and founded various schools, the first being in his native India.

The stimulating Moon-Sun-Mercury-Venus constellation signifies his teaching ability; he tried with the utmost perseverance (given by the fixed signs Taurus, Aquarius and Scorpio) to familiarize his listeners with his central concern (Mercury conjunct the Sun), deliverance from the I, and to call them to

consciouness of the self (green aspects of the stimulating constellation). Krishnamurti's tragedy, which he himself often
mentioned with an air of resignation, is that his gift as a teacher
bore so little fruit: the blue aspects that would have helped him
are missing from the constellation. He was constantly commu-
nicating with a public that eagerly sat at his feet waiting for him
to do the impossible—namely to hand them his own spiritual
knowledge on a plate.

Krishnamurti's Moon stands at the cusp of a fixed house
in the mutable sign Sagittarius (in conjunction with the galactic center 25° 24′); a painful position which imposed a mas-
sive weight of suffering on him, especially in his younger
years. For a temperament alive to a wider, unrestricted outlook (Sagittarius), the Theosophical training and the prodi-
gious hopes placed in him soon became a prison. Krishnamurti finally freed his sense of self (Moon) from the tight
confines of his world (Sun in 3rd house), but his letters bear
eloquent testimony to the tremendous conflict of loyalties (in
the 11th house one is loyal) by which he was torn. He discarded the alien destiny he had foisted on him earlier through
the Sun in the 3rd house, and, in the process, gained a new
and personal ideal, that of spiritual friendship (Aquarius on
the AC: the vetting of the individual development). He said in
a speech:

> But those who genuinely want to understand, who
> are on the watch, who seek the imperishable, the
> beginningless and endless, will close ranks with
> greater determination and become a threat to all that
> is unessential, to what is unreal, to the phantoms.
> And they will combine, will be aflame, because they
> understand. We must create such a community. That
> is my aim. In true friendship of this kind—which you
> do not seem to know—each has the will to cooperate.
> Not at the behest of some authority or in order to be

made safe but because they really understand and therefore live in the imperishable. This is greater than all worldly friends, than all sacrifices.[3]

The Age Point in Krishnamurti's Horoscope

We will now discuss the Age Point in Krishnamurti's chart. Table 4 on pages 130–131 shows the radix AP, and the dates discussed in the next section are highlighted on the table with arrows so students can readily follow along. Also pertinent to this discussion of Krishnamurti is figure 22 (see page 132), his lunar node horoscope. We have also included his lunar node Age Point (see Table 5 on page 133). The dates that are discussed in the text are also highlighted in Table 5 with arrows.

Dec. 1897

One of the most important persons in Krishnamurti's life was his brother, Nityananda, who accompanied him on his many journeys and was his closest friend and second self until he died of tuberculosis at age 28. When Nitya was born, the Age Point of Krishnamurti, who was then 3, made a fine trine to Jupiter-Mars, which augured well for a close, harmonious relationship between the brothers.

Jan. 1910

At the end of 1909, at 14½, he met Annie Besant and was initiated by her into the task of being a representative of the highest master. With a sextile to Mars and a semisextile to Pluto, the AP builds an information figure, making possible a first step in the direction of spiritual awareness.

---

[3]Krishnamurti, from a talk he delivered in Saanen-Gestad, Switzerland, in 1984. (English translation is mine. *Tr.*).

Table 4. Radix AP Table for Krishnamurti.

1895 / Age 0	1901 / Age 6	1907 / Age 12
28 Feb ⊻ ☊	12 May S 2	12 May S 3
9 May □ ☉	6 Jul □ G	5 Jun ✳ ♀
11 May S 1	2 Aug □ ☾	6 Jul ⊻ ☿
		23 Sep ☋

1896 / Age 1	1902 / Age 7	1908 / Age 13
7 Feb ✳ G	16 Feb □ ♀	29 Mar ☍ ♄
5 Mar ✳ ☾	17 Mar ✳ ☿	25 Sep ✳ ♃
24 Sep △ ♀	27 May ☊	
23 Oct □ ☿	14 Nov ⊼ ♄	

1897 / Age 2	1903 / Age 8	1909 / Age 14
5 Jan ✕	27 Apr □ ♃	26 Aug I 3
28 Jun △ ♄	27 Aug I 2	25 Oct ⊻ ♈
25 Aug I 1		
➡ 13 Dec △ ♃		

1898 / Age 3	1904 / Age 9	1910 / Age 15
15 Dec □ ♈	20 Apr ✳ ♈	➡ 6 Jan ✳ ♂
	26 Jun □ ♂	21 Jul ⊻ ♆
	21 Dec ✳ ♇	

1899 / Age 4	1905 / Age 10	1911 / Age 16
25 Jan L 1	25 Jan L 2	26 Jan L 3
21 Feb △ ♂	17 Jul ⊼ ☷	7 Mar ☍ ☷
22 Aug □ ♇	26 Nov ⊻ ☊	31 Jul ✳ ☊
		➡ 6 Oct ♂ ☉

1900 / Age 5	1906 / Age 11	1912 / Age 17
23 Mar △ ☷	27 Jan ⊻ ☉	26 Jul ⊼ G
6 Aug ♂ ☊	21 Oct △ G	24 Aug ⊼ ☾
7 Oct ✳ ☉	16 Nov △ ☾	⇨

S = Sign; G = Galachi Center; I = Invert Point; L = Low Point.

Table 4. (continued)

1913 / Age 18	1920 / Age 25	1926 / Age 31
30 Mar ⚲ ♀	➡ 19 Mar ♂ ♀	➡ 10 Feb ⊼ G
➡ 1 May ♂ ☿	24 Apr ⚲ ☿	13 Mar ⊼ ☾
12 May S 4	25 Jul ♋	27 Oct ⚲ ♀
2 Aug ⚷		29 Nov ✶ ☿

1914 / Age 19	1921 / Age 26	1927 / Age 32
16 Mar ⊼ ♄	28 Feb △ ♄	➡ 19 Feb ♌
20 Oct ⚲ ♃	26 Aug ∣ 5	27 Aug ∣ 6
	➡ 26 Sep ♂ ♃	➡ 4 Sep □ ♄

1915 / Age 20	1922 / Age 27	1928 / Age 33
27 Aug ∣ 4	➡ 30 Dec ⚲ ♈	10 Mar ⚲ ♃

1916 / Age 21	1923 / Age 28	1929 / Age 34
➡ 9 Feb ♂ ♈	➡ 25 Jan L 5	25 Jan L 6
7 May ⚲ ♂	25 Mar ♂ ♂	➡ 27 Apr ✶ ♈
➡ 29 Dec ♂ ♆	8 Nov ⚲ ♆	13 Jul ⚲ ♂

1917 / Age 22	1924 / Age 29	1930 / Age 35
25 Jan L 4	1 Aug △ ♁	2 Feb ✶ ♆
2 Oct ⊼ ♁		30 Sep □ ♁

1918 / Age 23	1925 / Age 30	1931 / Age 36
27 Mar □ ⚵	17 Jan △ ⚵	1 Mar ⊼ ⚵
16 Jun ⚲ ☉	6 Apr ✶ ☉	10 May □ ☉
	➡ 12 May S 6	12 May S 7

1919 / Age 24
12 May S 5
4 Jun ☍ G
9 Jul ☍ ☾

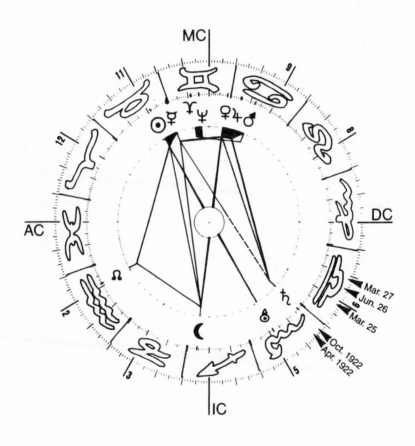

Figure 22.   The nodal chart for Krishnamurti.

Table 5. LN Age Point Table for Krishnamurti.

1913 /Age 18 3 Mar ⋏ ☉ 12 May S 4 12 May □ ☊ 9 Oct ⚻ ♄	**1919 /Age 24** 4 Mar ☍ ☉ 12 May S 5 12 May △ ☊ 9 Oct ☌ ♄	**1925 /Age 30** ➡ 3 Mar ⋏ ☉ 12 May S 6 12 May ⋏ ☊ 9 Oct ⚻ ♄
1914 /Age 19 2 Jun ☍ ♆ 21 Dec ⋏ ♂	**1920 /Age 25** 1 Jun ⋏ ♆ 20 Dec △ ♂	**1926 /Age 31** ➡ 2 Jun △ ♆ 21 Dec □ ♂
1915 /Age 20 6 Mar ☍ ♈ 27 Aug I 4	**1921 /Age 26** 6 Mar ⋏ ♈ 26 Aug I 5	**1927 /Age 32** ➡ 6 Mar △ ♈ 27 Aug I 6
1916 /Age 21 17 Apr ⋏ ♃ 19 Oct ⚻ ♄	**1922 /Age 27** ➡ 17 Apr △ ♃ ➡ 20 Oct ☌ ♄	**1928 /Age 33** 16 Apr □ ♃ 19 Oct ⚻ ♄
1917 /Age 22 25 Jan L 4 1 May ♐ 21 Jul ☍ ☿ 23 Aug ⋏ ♀	**1923 /Age 28** 25 Jan L 5 1 May ♏ 22 Jul ⋏ ☿ 23 Aug △ ♀	**1929 /Age 34** 25 Jan L 6 1 May ♎ 21 Jul △ ☿ 23 Aug □ ♀
1918 /Age 23 5 Apr ⚻ ☽	**1924 /Age 29** 4 Apr ⚹ ☽	**1930 /Age 35** 4 Apr □ ☽

Oct. 1911

The year 1911 was very important. Krishnamurti was 16 and his AP transited the Sun. "The Order of the Star in the East" was expressly founded for him in view of the role he had to play. In addition, he travelled to England for the first time with Annie Besant and his brother. One can imagine what a culture shock this was for the young orphan. In this portentous year,

the AP activated the ambivalent Sun-Uranus-lunar node constellation. What resulted was the sudden uprooting from the
homeland (Uranus 9th house) and the imposition of a life-task
within the context of the "Star" (Sun 3rd house).

May 1913

In 1913, when the AP transited Mercury, making a semisextile to Venus and a quincunx to Saturn, Krishnamurti came
to know Lady Emily, a motherly woman who gave him the
security and love he sorely missed. Unfortunately, they were
constantly being separated (the quincunx is a separation
aspect), which was a great trial to them.

Feb.-Dec. 1916

The passage of the AP over the Pluto-Neptune conjunction was
not marked by any spectacular events. But shortly afterward
Nityananda wrote a letter to Annie Besant in which he said:

> Krishna is incredibly altered. He can look into
> people's hearts [Neptune!] and is capable of making
> up his own mind. He stands much more firmly on his
> own feet than he did before, and although he is not
> aggressive and never will be, many folk are irritated
> by what they call his sudden obstinacy.[4]

This suggests that Krishnamurti had undergone a pro-
found inner change. Obviously he had acquired a spiritual
(Neptune) authority (Pluto) of his own. The evidence appears
in the fact that from this time forward he ceased to give blind
assent to the proposals of the Theosophical Society and also
voiced open criticism of his teacher, Leadbeater.

---

[4]Pupul Jayakar, *Krishnamurti: A Biography* (New York: Harper & Row, 1986).
(English translation is mine. *Tr.*)

Sept. 1921

During the passage of the AP over Venus and Jupiter, Krishna-murti spent a very happy and easy time. He led in command-ing style the first "Star" World Congress, gave many lectures and travelled a good deal. In the autumn of 1921, he briefly fell in love (AP conjunct Jupiter), but sexual relations, marriage and a family of his own had no further appeal for him.

LP 5

On August 20, 1922, when he was 27, he underwent a com-plete change of life. As a result of intense meditation and in great physical pain, he experienced Samadhi (absorption in the divine) for the first time. Although the Age Point was transiting Low Point five (exact in January 1923), it was making no special aspect at this time apart from a weak semisextile to Pluto.

LN-AP Oct. 1922

In view of this dearth of radical aspects, I took a look at his lunar mode horoscope and found that the lunar node AP had reached Saturn and was activating the Saturn-Jupiter trine directed at the 9th house region of religious knowledge. Appar-ently, that summer, Krishnamurti burst through the bounds of his earthly existence as it was at that time. From then on, under great physical suffering (Saturn) he at last brought to maturity the spiritual fruit (trine) that had been in him from birth.

May 1925 Cusp 6

At the end of 1925 his brother Nityananda died. This loss finally shook his confidence in the Theosophical psychics who had predicted a recovery, and represented a significant stage in Krisnamurti's detachment from the world-view of the Theosophists. In *March 1925*, the LN-AP formed a quincunx to the Sun, and in *March 1926*, the radical AP formed a quincunx to the Moon and to the Galactic Center. This represents the feelings of pain and longing for his dead brother. But the aspect does not explain the inner change that took place in Krishnamurti afterward, a change he expressed in the following words:

> A dream is dead and a new dream is born, like a flower thrusting up through the hard soil. A fresh vision has taken shape and a new consciousness has to unfold with it. . . . My brother and I are one. As Krishnamurti I now possess greater enthusiasm, greater faith, greater compassion and greater love, for in me now is also the body, the being of Nityananda. . . . I can still weep, but that is human. I now know with greater certainty than ever before, that there is real beauty in life, real happiness, which is not capable of being destroyed by physical happenings, that there is great strength which is not weakened by passing events and a great love that is lasting, imperishable and invincible.[5]

Jun. 1926

A glance at the Lunar Node-AP reveals that in June 1926 there was a trine to Neptune—the freeing from limitations of Krishnamurti's ego through this death: there is no aspect more appropriate to the release of transcendental love and boundless compassion.

Feb. 1927

Again, the most crucial action of his life, his public declaration rejecting the teachings of the Theosophists together with the

---

[5]Jayakar, *Krishnamurti: A Biography*. (English translation is mine. *Tr.*)

role they had intended for him, is not clearly mirrored by the radical AP: of course, the sign change from Cancer to Leo did give him the inner confidence to go his own way; but this "Plutonic turning point" would not have been sufficiently motivated by the sign change, in my opinion, even allowing for the square to Saturn that is due a little later.

Mar. 1927

But now look at the Lunar Node-AP: in the same spring of 1927 it makes an exact trine to the Pluto-Neptune conjunction. In the lunar node horoscope this stands at the MC. The spiritual independence that Krishnamurti had always had deep down now completely broke through and from then on he struck out on his own. As a direct result he dissolved the "Star" and left the Theosophical Society at the end of 1929.

Apr. 1929

This move coincided with a sextile of the radical AP to the Pluto-Neptune conjunction. After the great inner change, which culminated with the trine of the Lunar Node AP to Pluto, this sextile gave Krishnamurti the impulse to act positively and to take the external consequences.

A comparison of the Lunar Node AP and the radical AP shows that the milestones in Krishnamurti's progress since the great change, the Samadhi experience, are better represented by the Lunar Node AP. Apparently, the decisive conscious impulses came from stored experiences and led Krishnamurti's spirituality to a very high degree of development.

The following is his felicitous description of the concerted action of inner and outer (nodal chart):

> When we see what goes on in the world, we begin to understand that there are no outer and inner processes, but only a single unitary process, an all-

embracing motion, whereby the inner motion is exhibited in the outer and the outer reacts in turn on the inner. To my mind, the ability to look is all that is required; for, when we know how to look, everything becomes perfectly clear. And this act of looking needs no philosophy, no teacher. No one has to tell you how to look. You just look.[6]

And the esoteric seed thought of his Sun sign Taurus is: "I see, and when the eye is opened all is illumined."[7]

---

[6]Krishnamurti, *Freedom from the Known* (New York: Harper & Row, 1969), p. 16.
[7]Louise Huber, *Reflections and Meditations on the Signs of the Zodiac* (Tempe, AZ: American Federation of Astrologers, 1984), pp. 46.

Chapter Eight

Low Point Experiences:
Twelve Gates to the Spiritual Life

Today more and more people are being influenced by the laws of spiritual progress. Many are taking an interest in esoteric, parapsychological or religious topics: they long for peace, freedom and guidance, for a guru to show them the way. They are fascinated by spiritual questions, even to the extent of neglecting everyday affairs, and so get themselves into great difficulties and developmental crises. Therefore it is necessary for psychologists, astrologers, physicians, educators, and those who want to help others to know something about the laws of spiritual development, in order to be able to understand the needs of those seeking advice and to give them effective support. And here is where Age Progression can give considerable assistance.

The intention of the present chapter is to explain the significance of the twelve Low Point positions in spiritual development. Since this is a wide field, we shall look at it from different angles.

Cycles and Intermissions

The Low Point experience is something of an intermission between two cycles. Technically speaking, this experience has to do with the division of the houses into a cusp region and a Low Point region (peak and valley). The two cycles, descending and ascending, show up clearly on the intensity curve (figure 27 on page 158). The curve changes direction and rises again at the Low Point.

The changeover from one region, or condition, to another involves a brief stop preparatory to moving upward; and this happens every three years and eight months after the crossing of a house cusp. At the passage of the Age Point through the Low Point, we nearly always have a feeling of standstill, and often of stagnation. The spell of external activity and success we enjoyed at and after the cusp has petered out. Nothing seems to be going on, we are just marking time. Also there is a perceptible inward pull, because the Low Point may be seen as the point of ingress to the center of our being. A phase of introversion begins, usually lasting from eight to twelve months. We call this a Low Point year.

Our own life, like the life of nature, does not solely consist of alternate phases of building up and breaking down; in between come shorter or longer pauses as we go into reverse. We are all familiar with the cycles of ebb and flow, of the passing of active day into inactive night, of breathing in and out, of the many things in life that come and go. These processes are typical of the course of events in nature's three kingdoms. In our conscious experience of these cycles and of the breaks between them, we reach at the Low Point a neutral place that is neither one extreme nor the other, a place from which we can survey and restructure our lives.

At each Low Point we get an opportunity to turn inward, to regain composure, to gather strength for the climb to the next cusp. The time of apparent rest at the Low Point is really a time of reorientation. With any change, something inside us always has to come to an end. New springs from old as the outworn is discarded. What is new is welcome because full of potential. The cycle is one in which no phase is quote like any that went before. Instead it forms a spiral in which crises constantly recur at higher levels. This spiral has its individual rhythm, oscillation or pulse, with intermittent pauses, having a cosmic, and therefore a spiritual, significance. What we are saying can be made clear in *A Treatise on White Magic*, by Alice A. Bailey:

> God breathes, and His pulsating life emanates from the divine heart and manifests as the vital energy of all forms. It flows, pulsing in its cycles, throughout all nature. This constitutes the divine inhalation and exhalation. Between breathing out and the breathing in comes a period of silence and the moment for effective work. . . . With the manner in which this One Life of the solar system works in these vast interludes of meditative silence, called technically a pralaya, we need not concern ourselves. . . . What does concern the student of these Instructions however is how he can himself attain a definite constructive activity in *his* interludes.[1]

When we learn to make good use of this intermediate time we can achieve great inner freedom.

Spiritual Meaning of Low Point Stations

The Low point stations have a deep spiritual significance, even for our own small lives. They pull us up short, and present us

---

[1] Alice A. Bailey, *A Treatise on White Magic* (New York: Lucis Publishing Co., 1987), pp. 512-513.

with an opportunity for spiritual development. During this respite, we become aware of our own depths; we return to base, to a safe retreat where we can relax before pursuing the upward way like one reborn. The Low Point puts us in touch with the soul, the center of our innermost being, and gives us strength to press onward. These intermissions have much in common with the contemplative state in which the "Light of the Soul" enters our awareness. By cultivating this illumination or intuition, call it what you will, we enable our inner life or pure self—which gradually unfolds during recurrent Low Points—to become a determining factor in our existence and therefore in our environment.

Those who are totally absorbed by the affairs of the busy world, or have few Low Point planets in their charts, almost never appreciate the true nature of intermissions; their psyches could receive an unexpected jolt when braked by the inner self at such times. Judged by our frantic activity, the self is relatively motionless. Not for nothing has it been called the point of absolute stillness and peace. Most people are always in a hurry, they are always doing something, rushing here and there, so preoccupied that they have no time to think of anything else but their duties, their jobs, their money-making and so on. Each Low Point calls a halt, inviting them to come to their senses. Before the Low Point is reached, the fixed region of a house has to be traversed, beginning at the Invert Point. Right here is where a person of sense will consider slowing down instead of stepping up the pace of an already hectic life. Whoever eases off at this stage, ignoring outside pressures, and starts to look within will also be able at the Low Point to hear the inner voice of the true self and, in general, to perceive things not previously experienced.

Those who have given no thought to the inner world would profit from a perusal of the available books on the subject. Because a transformation does occur at the Low Point, whether we know it or not, it is better to turn this to our advantage than to try to fight it with our small egos. The more we balk, the sharper will be the crisis. Nowadays a growing number of people are concerned with spiritual development and with living in conformity with natural law. And many are professionally active in spiritual and psychological fields as therapists, astro-psychological counsellors, teachers of meditation and the like.

This desire for inner development is none other than the force of evolution directly operating through the will of the self at the Low Points. The universe evolves through us and, at the Low Points, we need to cultivate calm, open the inner ear, and respond cheerfully. By assisting evolution we improve our understanding of the inner self and contribute to progress. Those who are already sensitive to spiritual vibrations, possibly having several planets (especially the personality planets, Sun, Moon and Saturn) at the Low Points, are already alive to these experiences and, when the AP transits a Low Point, will make intense contact with their inner selves and will become the recipients of genuine guidance, insight and knowledge. Many have a vision and inner conviction of immediate goals, experience a new state of consciousness, discover a source of inner strength enabling them, at the next cusp, to achieve the goals that have now become clear. They know that, in the period that is astrologically represented by the climb to the cusp, they will have to put their ideals about themselves and the world into some viable form reflecting their new awareness. By integrating inspirations, concepts, and motivations, they can cooperate with their true will; gaining in the process deep inner satisfaction, more joy of living, better health, and a fresh purpose. They can feel the unity of all life, and can approach the inner self as a copy of the universe and a sacred shrine.

This sense of unity ought to become a permanent feature of our consciousness, and should be treated — not as something to be sampled briefly at the Age Point — but as something that can permanently color our mental attitudes. When it does so, many problems will vanish of their own accord.

In Low Point experiences, we are essentially coming into contact with the inner self and with live spiritual energies. We experience, perhaps for the first time, the magnitude of the oneness of all life and see ourselves as a reflection of something higher, as a microcosm of the macrocosm. We acknowledge the great law "as above so below" and understand that we are engaged in continual give and take with a larger life of which we form part and from which we derive our being.

It may be a pleasant or, on the other hand, a staggering thought, that our own small parcel of energy shares in the cyclic energy flow of this immense cosmic space or entity. The experience of all-pervading energy and of the synthesis of the One Life is typical of the Low Point at a higher level. Incidentally, the unity of human and God is a ubiquitous religious idea and a ground of ancient astrology.

The Circle in the Center

Let's look at the horoscope from another direction. We are familiar with the houses, signs, and aspects, and we know of the circle in the center symbolizing the self. This center has many names: some call it the soul, psyche, anima or atman; others call it the spirit, higher self, or monad. In fact it does not matter what we call it. What does matter is the realization that this self, as life-giver and governing factor, is the starting point and end point of our life, and that we can discover something about it during the transit of the Low Point. See figure 23.

The self is the creative power that gives birth to the personal I, that sustains it during a lifetime, and then retires into itself. We can think no thought and draw no breath without its aid. The self is the hub of the wheel on which all the spokes of body, mind, and emotions converge. In the horoscope, it is the

Figure 23.   The Circle in the Center.

circle in the center. When it appears, the native first begins to be. That is to say, it represents the existence of the native and the impulse behind his or her personal development. The problem posed by the Low Point experiences of life is to find and to travel the road back to the self, the circle in the center; or, in other words, the road back to origin. The urge to go to the point from which we came and to which we return is as old as humanity itself.

We can visualize life energy pouring into the horoscope out of this circle in the center, and supplying life and strength to the planets that serve us as organs of expression. The planets, for their part, receive from the cosmic qualities of the signs energies from space that — channeled through the qualities of the individual self — can reach the environment through the house system.

The process is an eternally pulsing exchange — an inbreathing and outbreathing in unison, so to speak, of human and cosmos. This energy exchange is full of mystery, and discloses the riddle of human existence and of creation. The subtle radiations of the self are etheric and stream through all forms of life. It follows that the self comes from the same life-substance as the great world in which we live and the nature of which we share.

Experiencing the Horoscope Through Meditation

The simplest approach to the self is to experience the horoscope through meditation. This method is fairly new, and has the character of self-initiation because one identifies meditatively with one's personal horoscope and thus with one's own being.

People who are trained in meditation or who can use their powers of visualization should consciously place themselves at the center of their own chart. If, then, in the mind's eye, they let the horoscope circle them (after they have studied it well), and imagine that the Ascendant is on the left, the Descendant on the right, the planets will suddenly light up all round as living forces. See figure 24.

Meditation Exercise

In this exercise we withdraw mentally from the outside world of the houses, pass through the zodiac belt, leave behind us the planets or psychic forces and—in the field of consciousness represented by the aspect configuration—locate the still eye in the perpetual whirl of thought, a place of deepest peace and unbroken silence.

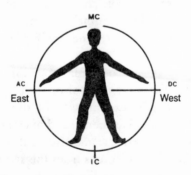

Figure 24.   Experiencing the horoscope as a meditation.

When we place our consciousness in the center of the chart, we see a bright point, shining like the sun. We identify ourselves with this point. Undulatory beams move outward in all directions from this point; and the first thing they fall on is the aspect configuration, since this is something that inwardly preoccupies us. For example, we are well aware of "that square" in our chart and know exactly where to look for it; so, every time it is struck by the inner light, it flashes like an electric filament under high tension. This must surely tell us something about the nature of the aspect.

The blue trines and sextiles are slack, like clotheslines. They sway from side to side under the impact of the imagined inner light, harmoniously following its flow. The quincunx, or long green aspect, is like a thin glass tube in which the inner light is reflected in rainbow colors. It is sometimes called "the yearning aspect," and encourages fantasies, wishes and projections; until, that is, we realize that we come to know something of the light by looking more closely at these reflections of the self. Once we identify a ray of truth, we are in a position to pursue the inner quest. The long green aspect then becomes a decision or will aspect and leads to spiritual growth.

The oppositions are like extended shining iron bars; they are rigid, hard and strong. As they stand like girders in space, the energies of the inner self course along them and make them glow brightly. They conduct these energies very intensely but unidirectionally, according to their polarity. If another planet is present, forming two squares (one to each of the planets in opposition), we get the T-square, which is full of tension and of energies that can make for success.

The aspect configuration should be studied with the inner eye again and again; only then ought we to move on to the planetary influences. When we do, the first thing we notice is that the planets at the Low Points are considerably nearer to us than those at the house cusps are. The cusp planets lie much further away from the center of consciousness. We have tried to illustrate this in figure 25 on page 148.

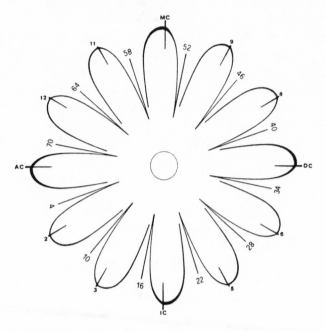

Figure 25.   The Low Points—channels to the inner center.

There is a direct route from one's innermost being to the Low Points. Any planet standing at one of the latter is brightly illuminated by the center and is a vital connecting force. When, for example, Uranus stands at the Low Point of a house, it can be contacted directly; the higher mind has a powerful influence, and the meditative approach to the inner center is easy to use. And when, to take another example, Saturn is directly reached by the energies of the self, that is to say, when it stands at a Low Point, then its transit by the Age Point is usually signalled by a desperate situation along the lines of the house theme. Saturn then acts as the Dweller of the Threshold, and calls for the death of old forms — something often bewildering and very painful. Crystallized behavior patterns are corrected and made less stiff, and may even be destroyed—all in the interests of clearing the way for further harmonious development.

Since the life center radiates so powerfully, the aspects need to act as transformers for the inner currents. Their network, as seen by our inner eye during horoscope meditation, vibrates in various colors. The glowing currents that run through it bring about an exchange of vital energy between the planets, and a differentiation in our consciousness. The aspects are thought-structures, by means of which we assimilate our experiences in the outside world and by means of which we can react on the outside world. Conversely, from the standpoint of the self, it is these thought structures and mental processes that the self ingests as experience and stores in the so-called causal body as essence for incarnation.

This visible representation of consciousness is in perpetual motion, and when seen as a medium transmitting the life-energy of the individual, it lies nearest to the self. On the other hand, looked at from the outside, the aspect configuration is furthest removed from human consciousness. Can any of us say that, at this moment, he or she is consciously working on the mental plane? Few indeed; and formerly such activity was reserved for initiates. Although on this mental plane we can now understand and control our thought-structure much better, we are still far from building up thought forms consciously and beneficially.

As we have seen, the fierce activity of the living flame is moderated by the aspect structure before it meets the outside world; which is just as well, for the central energy of the life or will is like a consuming fire, to use a Biblical phrase. The more aspects there are, the more differentiated the consciousness, the more intense the thinking, the more suitable the energies that reach the outside world: but also the more laborious the development of thoughts and ideas.

There is always the possibility that there are simply no aspects leading outward from the center point. We all know horoscopes with lacunae; in these the environment has direct access to the center of the being and, when the Age Point passes over such holes, the self is touched on a raw spot.[2]

Frequently an entire half of the chart is untenanted and open. This suggests a sort of uniform consciousness. In a sense, inner and outer are all one; they are not differentiated, are not consciously perceived as separate fields. One could say they exist in a kind of symbiosis in which no personal consciousness is possible. Also, in the sector concerned, there is little sharpness of identity. Thus the free energy flow is not particularly propitious; for the native reacts with less awareness in the given areas of life and fails to apply the forces of the self purposefully.

As already mentioned, it will be found that planets on the house cusps appear to be much further out from the center. Also they are much less under the control of the central energy; being outward-looking, and absorbed, influenced and used by the external world. This is in contrast to planets at the Low Point, or even at the Invert Point, which are much nearer to the central force and can convey spiritual energies.

If you will perform the exercise, you will be amazed at what fresh discoveries you can make about your horoscope. This method of visualizing from within is good training for intuition; in fact, we may as well call it "intuitive astrology." Its advantage is the direct experience it gives of what is usually a formal, external, intellectual, mercurial knowledge of the planets, aspects, and signs.

We shall now outline a form of meditation that can be used privately or in self-awareness groups. After the actual meditation, it has been found useful for group members to exchange notes on their mental images and experiences in order to get as much out of them as possible.

---

[2]Further reference to this will be found in *Lifeclock Volume 2* in the chapter on rules of interpretation.

Horoscope Meditation

Sit comfortably in a chair with eyes closed and allow yourself to glide into a state of tranquility and relaxation. Let all your muscles relax until there is no tightness anywhere. Direct your attention to your brow muscles to make sure they are no longer taut. Your forehead should be smooth, your expression friendly, and your tongue should lie in the lower jaw. Breathe quietly and evenly through the nose. As you inhale think, "Breathing is within me," and surrender yourself to the rhythm of the breath — in and out, in and out.

1st Stage:
The Circle in the Center

Concentrate your consciousness in the head and then let it sink slowly in the middle of the body, through the jaw, neck, and upper chest. Allow your consciousness to come to rest in the chest and picture a golden white sun rising in the heart center. This is the central part of your being; in the horoscope it is the circle in the center. Install yourself here, and feel yourself securely anchored in this central place.

2nd Stage:
Personality Finding

Take a look at your horoscope. On the left is the AC, on the right the DC, below you is the IC, above you the MC. Next visualize the personality planets: the Sun, Moon, and Saturn, arranged exactly as in your birth chart. First turn your attention to the Sun; fetch it in close and examine it in relation to its sign, house and aspects. Then push it slowly back into the outer circle and fetch in the Moon, examining that in relation to its sign, house, and aspects. Slowly restore the Moon to its place in the chart and fetch in Saturn, seeing its symbol in the mind's eye. Examine the planet in relation to its sign, house and aspects before putting it back again.

These three planets are the pole of your personality. Together with the other planets they are the tools of your soul, with which you express yourself in, and impress yourself on, the world. Now let Mercury, Venus, Mars, Jupiter, and lunar nodes, the rising sign, and the higher planets Uranus, Neptune and Pluto come into mental view. Their positions in the horoscope are an expression of your own self. Recognize your chart and accept it for what it is.

3rd Stage:
Meditation on the Aspect Configuration—
Living Consciousness

Bury yourself in your chart, letting it expand and carry the planets over the horizon. You are now left with aspects exhibiting a variety of shining, pulsating, streaming colors.

The oppositions are long, red-hot girders, humming with fiery energy; they are set to point in one direction. The squares are red lines of force, vibrant with electric fire. The trines are light-tubes, in which a dense luminous blue flows quietly and soothingly. The green aspects are thinner and more flexible. A fluorescent green glow flashes swiftly up and down them. The conjunctions are like orange pools of static energy. You should stand at the central point and watch this brilliant play of light.

4th Stage:
Self-Awareness

Now retire deeper still inside yourself and see yourself as the source of your life, as the cause of everything. You are a center of sheer life and will energy. You are the constant, unchanging

Self and are in a position to stimulate, heal, guide, and use all the psychological processes in yourself and in your three bodies. Let the light of the golden white sun shine out from your heart on the aspect configuration, the planets, the signs, the houses, and out into your environment. Then contemplate: I am that and that is I.

Slowly withdraw from the state of meditation, breathe deeply in and out, open your eyes, and move your head, hands and feet.

•   •   •

This form of meditation can be altered to suit yourself. We would suggest that, if you are a beginner, you might start with two or three elements and add a few more each time the exercise is repeated. The planets and houses are easiest to visualize — their images spring into view straight away; whereas to see the aspect configuration takes a little practice.

So we have two paths that lead to the self: one is the direct route by which we identify with the circle in the center through meditation or imagination, the other is the path of life round the twelve houses, unfolding as they do the whole panorama of development from birth to death.

Breathing Rhythms

The way of self-awareness may also be illustrated by the function of breathing in and out. The run up to the house cusp is similar to breathing in. There is a short pause at the cusp; then, like breathing out, comes the glide down to the Low Point, where there is a further pause before the next breath is drawn. Movement ceases at the Low Point, for a moment all is still — then comes another inhalation. The respiratory rhythm (see figure 26 on page 154), resembling as it does the cyclic

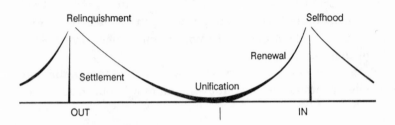

Figure 26. The breathing cycle.

course of the twelve houses, can tell us something about the meaning of the latter when put in the following terms — relinquishment, settlement, unification, renewal, selfhood.

The house cusp is abandoned in the spirit of letting go. Then, on reaching the Invert Point, it is time for us to settle down, since we are in the fixed region of the house where things are consolidated. At the Low Point, we hold our breath and think of unification. Next comes the indrawn breath of renewal and, finally, self-realization at the cusp.

Crises of Development and Awareness

As we have just seen in figure 26, unification has to do with the Low Point. The individual who has experienced mystical union and has come in contact with his or her inner self, or with the divine spark, would like nothing better than to have the experience continue. Unfortunately, for the most part, it quickly comes and goes and is not a permanent state. Therefore this individual sets out to recapture what has been lost, by becoming religious or taking up meditation, and is ready to make any sacrifice for the sake of progress on the path of spiritual improvement. This path is something we must think about if we wish to understand the crises of development and awareness arising at different stages in life. The path of spiritual improvement on which the individual has set out is a long track leading through strange places; it is full of wonderful experiences, but also of obstacles and dangers. It calls for thorough purging, a total transformation of the attitude to life, the awakening of previously inaccessible abilities, the raising of consciousness to new heights, and the acquisition of new motives. These things tend to come to the fore when Low Points are transited; although, obviously, not without trauma.

Someone who has been absorbed in material and social matters may be surprised and alarmed by a sudden eruption of spiritual life as one of the Low Points is passed. Often such experiences are due to disappointments, or mental shock — for example, from the loss of someone close. Those who have been exposed to the forces of change exerted by the self can no longer devote themselves entirely to looking after their physical needs. All the personal details that have so far absorbed their attention lose importance. Getting what they want is no longer a thrill. They begin to ponder over the meaning of life and over the causes of many phenomena they used to take for granted. They ask questions about the sufferings of themselves and others and about the origin and purpose of human existence in general. And this is where misunderstanding and error creep in.

Many do not understand the reason for their new state of mind worry that they are suffering from morbid fancies and struggle hard to get rid of them. Out of fear that the ground is going to give way beneath them, they do everything imaginable to return to solid reality. They throw themselve with redoubled energy, almost in desperation, into the whirl of life and avidly seek new occupations, fresh attractions, and novel sensations. By these means they succeed in calming their unrest for a time, but seldom in removing it indefinitely. The transforming forces of the soul remain active in the depths of their being, undermining the foundations of their everyday life, and can—even after several years—break out again with renewed violence, usually at the next Low Point.

Frequently, a moral and ethical crisis occurs, and the individual no longer knows what is right or wrong, but gets lost in relative values and is unable to keep a firm grip on absolute standards. What once was good can now be bad. The individual starts living beyond good and evil. Altogether this is a difficult period, esoterically known as "the dark night of the soul." The old order has ended and the new has not yet begun. The inner life matures slowly. The process is long and complicated, consisting of phases of active cleansing to remove hindrances that block the flow and effectiveness of the spiritual forces, of phases when there is a development of inner abilities that formerly were hidden and weak, and of phases when the personality is quiescent, allowing a spiritual work to take place while it bears unavoidable suffering with courage and patience. It is a time of change, in which light and darkness, pleasure and pain alternate.

A reaction usually sets in after a period of spiritual growth, because habitual modes of behavior operate like an automatic mechanism to draw the person back into old routines. Here we have another case of "it always gets worse before it gets better." Everything unwished-for appears *en masse*, the individual thinks that no progress has been made at all and quickly loses heart. But fresh courage must be taken and renewed efforts made to consolidate the changes. After the first few steps on the path of spiritual development, there is no going back.

Many people nowadays find themselves on the spiritual path and needing help, mostly in the form of understanding, encouragement and reassurance. When we see what the Age Point is doing, and realize that in this position it gives expansion of consciousness and spiritual development, then we can show the inquirer that there is a deeper meaning in his or her experience—however painful it may have been. Only the knowledge that it is part of progress can bring the individual back in unity with the regulatory laws of nature, and put the necessary distance between the self and the problems, so that new positive qualities of life are set free. Often a single astrological consultation is enough to give the native a fresh outlook plus the courage to trust in the inherent forces of development. When shown that progress is a stage-by-stage affair and that crises of consciousness necessarily occur at the Low Points, he or she can adopt a different attitude to problems, and can see the causal connection of the latter so they can be integrated in the life. Over the years, as consultants and teachers, we have had the opportunity to observe hundreds of examples of this liberating, neutralizing and healing action.

However, in some cases these crises really unsettle the psyche, often producing the same symptoms as neurosis, schizophrenia or other mental diseases. Roberto Assagioli, the founder of psychosynthesis, made a special study of the relationship between nervous disorders and spiritual development, and from this has come transpersonal psychology. We have incorporated this knowledge in our astrological concept.

In the horoscope, there are many forms of approach to the path of spiritual progress. The most important is Age Progression, as this shows how the I unfolds. The way through the zodiac signs provides another important clue to the inquirer, which is discussed in detail elsewhere.[3] Also the position of the Dragon's Head in the twelve houses is a point of ascent for the spiritual path. But the twelve Low-Point stations place in our hands a real key to the effect of change on the ego and on the spiritual aspirant — especially when they are taken in conjunction with the qualities of the three crosses (cardinal, fixed and mutable).

---

[3]See Louise Huber, *Reflections and Meditations on the Signs of the Zodiac* (Tempe, AZ: AFA, 1986).

The Three Crosses and the Transmutation of the Ego

As we know, the crosses have to do with deep human motivations or, in other words, with why a person behaves in one way
and not in another. The ego is closely identified with these
motivations, for without them it cannot live: it needs a moving,
motivating force to be able to exist. Therefore the qualities of
the three crosses are very enlightening when we come to consider the various stages of development and the ego-trans-
formations at the Low Points. The qualities of some two different crosses will be found to meet at the various Low Points.
This can be seen in the following intensity curve (see figure
27). It will be observed that the curve rises from the deepest
point to the cusp, then falls again. What this means is that a
house really starts at the Low Point, that the cusp is its strongest region, and that it ends at the next Low Point. This is what
we call the dynamic house system.

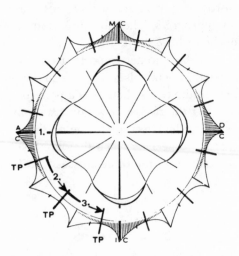

Figure 27.   The intensity curve.

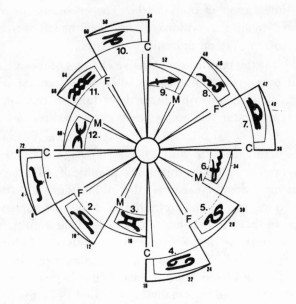

Figure 28. The three crosses. C = cardinal, F = fixed, and M = mutable.

As we say, in assessing the transformational qualities of the ego, we have to remember that Low Points are meeting places for different crosses with different qualities. This supplies the key to correct interpretation. When, for example, we wish to assess the transformational quality of the Low Point in the 1st house, we have to start from the fact that a change takes place here from cardinal to fixed, for the 2nd house (fixed) really starts at Low Point one (cardinal). The qualities of the cardinal and fixed crosses meet and produce a motivation here. Again, the cardinal 4th house starts at mutable Low Point three, and so the mutable cross gives way to the cardinal. The same principle applies to the rest of the houses. Where two types of motivation collide, change is bound to occur.

When cardinal gives way to fixed, the will becomes less expansive and self-consciousness is suitably deflated. A clash of fixed and mutable results in a loss of certainty and stability—

the disintegration of one's world. The encounter of mutable and fixed means that options can no longer be left open but one has to concentrate on one thing.

This is the reason why decisive changes of motive accompanied by corresponding crises often take place at the Low Points. We shall describe these more fully in relation to the three crosses and the twelve houses. See figure 28 on page 159.

In figure 28 (see also Plate 4 on page 100), we have endeavored to represent this theme graphically. The signs that project most are the cardinal, the middle signs are the fixed and the innermost signs are mutable. The same applies to the houses, so that the first house begins with the sign Aries. On the outer rims the Low Points are marked by small arrows and the progressed age. Just to remind the reader: on a more dynamic view of the houses, each house begins at the Low Point of what would normally be regarded as its predecessor.

The Cardinal Cross

Aries	Cancer	Libra	Capricorn
1st	4th	7th	10th house
4th	22nd	40th	58th year of life
			Low Point experience

As we all know, the cardinal cross produces an impetus that rises to a point of success or break-through, then subsides before gathering strength for a new effort. Its counterpart in the house system is the cusp. From the standpoint of development, this cross is typified by mental and spiritual drive, by individualism and the desire for self-realization, and by shows of strength. It brings the creative power of the will into play. The *Sun* is its ruler.

The cardinal "I" asserts its identity by mastering and controlling forms, objects and people. If one had a majority of cardinal signs and houses he or she is intent on using the will, on proving his or her strength, and impressing it on others, or on getting his or her own way. Everything is measured by will, vigor, and performance. At the cardinal-house Low Points, get-up-and-go forsakes him or her and inner powerlessness and ego-loss are suffered through. The test comes when he or she fails to achieve some goal. This individual makes plans that will take some time to materialize but he or she expects to see results right away. Having to wait tries the patience and failure is seen as a bitter personal defeat. It is the crushing realization that personal strength is not enough that begins the inner change. Then comes the surrender to a Higher Power, saying, "Lord, not as I will but as You will." This makes it possible to be at one with the central will of Being. This person may feel called to work for the Higher Power in the interests of making a better world. The personality gains an inspirational quality that points self and others to spiritual goals.

However, if the individual doesn't stand the test but reacts badly at the Low Point, if he or she is excessively proud and arrogant, if the personal "I" is obdurate and imagines it can do everything alone, the individual may become misguided enough to resist the growth of the inner self and to cut away from its vital forces. A barrier is errected between self and life. The energies of the self at the Low Point dash against these stiff walls of the ego. The more the native is wrapped up and encapsulated in the self, the more likely he or she is to suffer the crisis of a mental and physical breakdown. What is required is to recognize that, in the long run, worldly success can never satisfy the inner need; indeed, anxiety, misgivings and emptiness often increase with the growing envy and admiration of others. The sole solution is a drastic reversal—usually possible only when, out of sheer desperation, the individual calls for higher help and guidance, abandons self and becomes open to spiritual things. In transpersonal psychology, this has been given the name of the "Damascus road experience" in which a Saul can become a Paul,[4] and lets the personal will fall in line with the Divine Will, applying itself to worthwhile goals that promote progress and abandoning goals that are egotistical.

At the Low Points in the cardinal houses, one reaches one's limits. The correct response is to pull back and to concentrate on doing what is feasible; then success is possible.

The following are brief descriptions of Low Point experiences in the cardinal houses. No more than one or two points can be covered in the space available, so it is necessary to emphasize the importance of the signs in which the Low Points appear. These must be combined with the house qualities, because they can considerably affect, and even alter, the experiences (see chapter 2, "House/Sign Combinations in the Crosses").

In the 1st cardinal house in the 4th year of life we reach the obstinate or defiant age; the child sets itself against the will of its parents and has to learn that adults are stronger than he or she is. If the child is obedient, all should go well, and he or she will respect the territory of others and will always be able to recognize his or her own.

In the 4th cardinal house in the 22nd year of life the years of childhood and adolescence usually come to a close. The young person wants to live his or her own life and leaves the secure parental home in order to be independent. On becoming self-supporting, he or she discovers that coping alone is not as

---

[4]Saul was changed from a persecutor to a Christian by a vision of Jesus on the Damascus road. Some years later, when an apostle in Cyprus, he is said to be "also called Paul" (Acts 9 & 13). *Tr.*

easy as it looked. It often happens that, for selfish reasons, the young adult declines to leave; however, this can end in family rows that push the reluctant fledgling out of the nest.

In the 7th cardinal house in the 40th year of life the middle of life is already passed. One stands at the parting of the ways. Relationship with the environment and with one's fellow men and women should be harmonious and well-ordered and capable of resulting in a genuine partnership. Often, when partnerships are unsatisfactory, this is the age at which they are dissolved. It is also the age when one can be let down by the partner, when one can wait in vain for understanding, sympathy and cooperation, and yet be incapable of escaping from the partner. But whoever is ready for a true partnership or aspires to serve the community can enter a new sphere of activity at the Low Point of the 7th house.

In the 10th cardinal house in the 58th year of life one has passed the peak of life's expectations. Genuine authority in some field must already be ours if we are to work in harmony with the forces of individuation. Anyone who is still locked in competition with others will grimly hang on to the positions already won. But such a person will be lonely and will live in constant dread of being ousted, of being replaced by new blood. Those possessing genuine authority, on the other hand, will help to prepare the way for the young, will lead and guide them and attend to their promotion.

The Fixed Cross

Taurus	Leo	Scorpio	Aquarius
2nd	5th	8th	11th house
10th	28th	46th	64th year of life
			Low Point experience

This is the cross of fixation, of dogged clinging to gains and guarantees that only have to be given up in the end. The fixed cross causes certain big crises to do with the law of inertia and the process of detachment. Natives with predominantly fixed houses and signs are acutely aware of their identity; therefore they anchor themselves firmly in the world. They stand fast and do not allow themselves to be thrust aside or influenced. They know their limitations, and the stronger the walls they manage to build around themselves, the safer they feel. Their integrity consists in the inviolability of a space in which the I is well established.

The trials that come at the Low Points in the fixed houses have to do with the vanishing of set boundaries and with disillusionment. When the walls that seemed safe are removed, it is as if a protective covering has been destroyed. The result is uncertainty, chaos, and wild anxiety that one will lose everything one has. This fear of loss causes the individual to clutch desperately at whatever has been acquired or is believed to be rightfully theirs.

The paramount influence in the fixed houses is Saturn, which plays a significant role as a tester in the processes of change, and as the Dweller of the Threshold. Fixed-cross crises are particularly painful and are part and parcel of the eternal dying and becoming. The Low Points are charged with meaning here, since they naturally share the quality of the fixed cross; so, when they are actually in a fixed house, the fixed effect is doubled.

At the Low Points in the fixed houses, a radically new attitude to life needs to be adopted to enable further development to occur harmoniously. These are real crossroads of fate, turning points that make big difference to our lives. In the face of losses of any kind we ought to recognize and accept that life is full of change and is a continual process of growth and development in keeping with natural laws, and that it unfolds according to cosmic order. The belief that all is well, that there is a good reason for everything, and that nothing is accidental, should be encouraged and maintained.

We must continually shake off our fears, break through the walls that threaten to stifle us, renounce the misconceived policy of "safety at all costs" and change our egocentric attitudes, so that we can pass beyond limitations of our own making in order to reach the true self—or, to change the metaphor, in order to vibrate on the same wavelength as the self. Therefore union with the innermost center at the Low Points implies a letting go, an abandonment, and often a destruction, of whatever binds us to the world. The process of development and the initiatory way require an elastic response to the never-ending changes of life.

Deliverance in the fixed cross lies in continually surmounting barriers until, at last, we are at liberty to make our own decisions. The recognition that what fetters us is unwarranted and arbitrary sets us free to face the new with confidence. Then the new no longer has to pry open our shut fast lives in order to reach us—a painful process—but is welcomed gladly. On our own initiative, and without a qualm, we expand beyond our old limits to find our true measure. No borders can confine the life inside us that knows how to be at one with the Whole.

In reality, this is the middle path, the "razor's edge." The truth is that this path is narrow and quite hard to find. All religions and philosophies refer to it. It is the famous eye of a needle through which one must pass,[5] also the "Noble Middle Path" of the Buddha, the fine line of demarcation between the polarized forces of our being, which can be found and preserved only by passionlessness and by high concentration and powers of discrimination.

---

[5]"It is easier for a camel to go through the eye of a needle than for a rich man to enter the kingdom of God. . . . Who then can be saved? . . . With men this is impossible; but with God all things are possible." (Matthew 19) *Tr.*

Moderation is the characteristic of the fully aware person in the fixed cross. Every deviation from the happy medium, every excess or deficiency, sets in motion the forces of the self, the personal center of gravity, to restore or preserve the balance. It is the harmonious union of inner and outer, the equilibrium between feeling and understanding, that are depicted in the sage-looking, ever peacefully smiling Buddha.

Of course, this virtue can also land us in a stagnant, apathetic condition, in which we desperately try to stay put purely from fear of loss. Those in particular who are undiscerning need some bad breaks to make them grow up and rouse themselves from their crystallized inactivity. In this case it is fate that produces the inner change — usually at the Low Points of the fixed houses at the corresponding age. Depending on the house and planetary positions, fate may well intervene with the death of a loved one, with the loss of position, career or money, with an illness or brush with death, or with something equally unsettling. In the fixed cross, the native has to adopt the right attitude and make a decisive switch to new goals.

This inner change or reorientation comes from an insight into the futility of all material things, none of which can be taken with us when we go. It involves the calm acceptance that everything is governed by wise laws, that we get what we deserve — neither more nor less. It enables us to put down roots in the deepest part of our soul, having cut material ties in exchange for inner strength and certainty.

Development in the fixed cross comes from respecting the law of economy, by taking, accepting, and giving. In other words, through not trying to grab what we have not earned or what others have got. We must learn to be content. Then we can really appreciate our possessions and can be happy.

At the Low Point in the fixed houses, karma often suddenly comes into play: things to which we have no right are wrenched from our grasp; or the equilibrium is restored by privileges being given to some who have never dared to ask for them. At this time, everything is being evened up and Justice is busy with her balance. If we turn a deaf ear to fate and to the voice of conscience telling us to let go and share what we have, if we fail to devote ourselves to a higher order of things, we are bound to suffer for it.

This is where we need to accept that there are others to be considered besides ourselves. A clear understanding of what is meant by equal rights is a great help in fulfilling the requirements of the Low Points. Also the knowledge of what one is, of what one can be, and of what one has to offer the world is an aid to progress. It is no good feeling hard done by, or envying others their status, circumstances and wealth, unless one wants to stand still or run round in circles. True, the testing situations encountered in the fixed cross often tempt us into envy, covetousness and egotism; but a recognition of our own worth, assets and abilities should give us perspective, and enable us to act responsibly toward the greater whole. A liberating and healing power lies hidden in this cheerful self-acceptance. It removes the barriers which false pride and self-defense have erected between our fellow men and women, our inner spiritual forces, and us. Repeated refusals to give and persistent clinging to the past erect a fence that is impenetrable to the true self, and to the new and beautiful things that would come with it. Such negativism not only cuts us off from the forces of life, it is tantamount to tempting fate and opens a chapter of disappointments and reverses.

The thankful acceptance of one's lot is a direct route to those inner regions where the true self dwells. It restores the harmony between us and the higher powers that rule, protect and preserve us all, and so leads to a greater confidence in life.

Low Point experiences in the fixed cross always involve the nonfulfillment of personal aspirations, and often mark a time of disillusionment. What happens in the individual houses depends largely on the native's spiritual development and on the sign on the house cusp. The following are one or two possibilities.

In the 2nd fixed house at age 10, the child realizes that material possessions and clinging to the parents will give no security in the long run. The child is no longer very interested in these things and turns to other possibilities of self-establishment, open to new contacts and the give-and-take with children of the same age. School-work may prove burdensome.

In the 5th fixed house at age 28, there are changes affecting love-life and intimate contacts. Disappointments in professional and private life lead to reorientation. It is important to find one's own measure, one's own limitations, and to come to terms with reality. The genuineness of one's attitude is tested. Self-overestimation and faulty behavior are corrected by fate. The reckoning has to be paid.

In the 8th fixed house at age 45, there is a decisive change in the life-style, usually because of disillusionment. Many a glorious youthful dream finally fades away as we learn to deny ourselves and stick to our bargains. Facing reality and accepting destiny's decrees can be very painful, especially if we have set our sights high. Often our whole world collapses around us and life is forced onto a completely different road. Ties and obligations may feel like hardships from which there is no relief. Nothing seems to happen without a thorough shake-up and a great deal of destruction and reconstruction.

In the 11th fixed house at age 64, we have to slow down and bid farewell to hectic activity. A balance has to be struck, as we reconcile ourselves to the past and cheerfully accept what is still to come. The pensionable age is at the door, and if we do not steel ourselves against the fact that things are going to go on without us, we may suffer from retirement collapse, feeling isolated and thrown on the scrap heap. For many of us, therefore, it is important to forget the claims of the outside world and to prepare peacefully for the evening of life. The way to the Self and to one's inner being is then relatively easy and leads to tranquility, composure and contentment. Younger folk who see this will come and profit by our experience of life.

The Mutable Cross

Gemini	Virgo	Sagittarius	Pisces
3rd	6th	9th	12th house
16th	34th	52nd	70th year of life
			Low Point experience

 The mutable cross is the cross of love, of regular relationships, and of adaptation to form. It causes ceaseless change and periodic movements in time and space that offer suitable opportunities for the unfolding of the innermost being. The drive or motivation is the urge for love or friendship. In the mutable cross, the native has a continual longing deep down for affection, trust, sharing and mutual understanding. Time and again he or she loses love, time and again he or she sets out in search of love. The trek is endless.

In the mutable cross, one experiences one's identity as a point moving in time and space and free to form relationships with all other things. Any fixation usually results in a loss of identity and of the capacity for love; but these can be regained by letting go. There is a thirst for freedom, an avoidance of commitments and attachments, and an eager waiting for true love. One is ever seeking new contacts in order to make fresh discoveries about oneself and others.

The individual who has many planets (life functions) in mutable signs or houses goes looking for new people, places and situations, in the hope of experiencing love. The steady stream of new relationships helps the conscious mind to develop, and the native identifies with the law of development that he or she recognizes, under its many disguises, as the love principle behind evolution. The mutable cross is ruled by the *Moon*.

The tests, or Low Point experiences, typical of the mutable cross, consist of forfeiture of liberty, apparent loss of love, or the feeling of being misunderstood. There is less opportunity for wandering about with no fixed object in view—a decision has to be made in favor of something, even when this will be inhibiting. The restriction on movement is a difficult trial for the mutable cross and requires added depth of personality. One has to concentrate on a single issue, or make a commitment to one person. Limitations may be imposed from without and are then experienced as a compulsion or confinement. These are fiercely resisted until it is realized that they are necessary for preserving and protecting what has already been achieved, and for bringing stability into the life. The voluntary acceptance of sensible rules helps to make the conscious mind less shallow and erratic.

Absorption in some task, or the willingness to belong to another person, is a mark of progress in the mutable cross, and produces a greater responsibility towards life and its obligations—the very thing the native wishes to avoid at this stage, believing that love is experienced only in freedom. What awaits discovery is that it is possible when apparently caged, too.

At the Low Points one learns to accept responsibilities and to acknowledge the wisdom of laws regulating community life. Social behavior becomes central, and one is taught by experience how to fit in and contribute to the general good, even at personal cost. The need is for self-control, unremitting effort, and the highest devotion to spiritual ideals, so that love can survive in the daily grind or when an injustice is suffered. Mutual love cannot be taken for granted but must be accepted and cultivated; it needs constant attention. The love that men and women keep seeking through sacrifice, through adoration, through relationships, through sexuality, through every kind of lust, suffering and pleasure, can be found only when the past is entirely forgotten, when enemies are forgiven and one becomes like a child again, newborn and innocent. Then love has no opponent and is without conflict. But before all this, one has to reach lowest ebb, and, in sheer desperation, surrender oneself with one's hopes and fears. Then one is caught up to another plane, inhabited by the true self. In the final analysis, love is the power that flows from deep within, healing all wounds and restoring us to our center.

At the Low Points of the mutable houses, love is always the big issue; and it is important to give up any selfish demands for understanding, for gratitude, for fair play, for possessions, etc. As soon as such apparently justified claims have been renounced, one is immediately drawn to the center. What happens is like a sudden revelation from a higher dimension, an act of grace, an initiation, which revitalizes us and relieves us from care and distress. The moment one allows the self, and with it a love for all creatures, to flow out into the world, the world changes. If one can remain in this loving state, even in difficult circumstances, one will make uninterrupted progress and will keep being called to new tasks. The effect will be transforming, and the world and oneself will be seen in a different light. The insight can either catch one alarmingly off guard, or can become a perpetual source of cleansing and renewal.

Low-Point experiences in the mutable houses can briefly be described as follows. But note, they also depend on the zodiac signs through which the AP is passing.

In the 3rd mutable house at age 16, school days are usually over and professional training begins. The native has to decide what he or she is going to do. The sexual drive increases at the same time, but the desire for more freedom and for a personal love-life is usually misunderstood and curbed by trainers and educators. There are frequent rows with parents and superiors, and the young person is expected to toe the line. At the same time, he or she can start seeing the wider connections of things, and this can lead to a new awareness and to reorientation.

In the 6th mutable house at age 34, professional crises are common. Set-backs and defeats, not to mention health problems, necessitate an adjustment to objective reality, a trimming of plans for expansion, and the abandonment of illusionary dreams of the future. Often one finds at work that someone else is better than oneself; a decision has to be taken to join the community and concentrate on teamwork. Before the desired recognition can be gained, one has to be able to do or produce something. Many realize that they are in the wrong job, and start a fresh course of vocational training or strike out on a new road professionally.

In the 9th mutable house at age 52, there is a crisis of meaning. Everything seems to lose significance. All the experience and all the knowledge acquired so far now appear to be useless. But if one becomes empty, and admits one's own smallness and lack of power, the guiding impulse of the inner self can center consciousness and give it a new orientation. One must choose spiritual life, revive youthful ideals, and aim at unselfish goals that will benefit a wider circle. In this way life can take on a new meaning and human love can blossom again.

In the 12th mutable house at age 70 the physical and mental powers decline. Active life wanes. The time has come to think of the permanent side of oneself and to let the world go, in order to be at one with the true Self. People who are unable to cultivate inner detachment will feel lonely and deserted. The fear of death and what comes after can extinguish the joy of living and embitter them. But those who open up to the true Self enter a higher sphere, where it is possible to remain imperturbable. They can peacefully sever earthly ties, and can return serenely to the eternal REALITY from which they came.

APPENDIX

Rectification of the Birthtime

by Michael-A. Huber

To ascertain the correct time of birth in the absence of accurate data, key events in life can be compared with the movement of the Age Point through the chart. The procedure is simple: we inquire whether or not the events coincide with relationships of the Age Point to certain planets or aspects. If they do not, the birthtime must be wrong!

Not many birthtimes are correct, even when they have been taken from birth certificates. Therefore the house system must be moved clockwise or counterclockwise until its setting is exactly right.

Formerly, one had to juggle with progressed planets, solar arcs, and transits; calculating 10 to 20 moving points in the chart and comparing them with 8 to 15 dates in the life! With the Age Point, we keep track of only *one* moving point.

There is a big and important difference in the number of dates used: whereas traditional methods include literally all the available dates of significant events, in this new method we make do with some seven events that left their mark psycholog-

Figure 29.   An astrologer erecting a figure of the heavens. From a work of
Gautier de Metz, 13th century, The British Museum, London.

ically and altered the native's consciousness. This is because the Age Point describes the changes in consciousness that occur through life and indicates clear psychological themes. So, when you decide to carry out a rectification by means of the Age Point, special weight must be given to internal experiences, and to the mental changes or decisions that paved the way for external events. In conclusion, we shall work out the exact AP aspects of the sample horoscope, and so gain a better under-standing of the course taken by the life. In the process, some interesting relationships will be observed which could prove very instructive to the native. We recommend to each one, even when the exact birthtime is already known, to analyze his or her life in this way, using AP aspects that have already been formed.

The moments in which something happens inwardly are the cause of most of what later materializes. Take marriage for example: the decision to live together springs directly from the time when the two parties met and fell in love. Usually, the marriage opens their eyes to a new view of life. In that case, the Age Point is involved in a significant change of sign or aspect; otherwise, not.

Therefore, the thing to do, when experiences are being recounted, is to discover by careful inquiry which of them were the most intense, and most deeply affected the course of life. The accuracy of the rectification of a time of birth depends on three factors:

1) The available number of psychologically signifi-cant dates.

2) The accuracy of these dates.

3) The size of the margin of possible birthtimes.

The bigger the span of time we have to allow for the possible occurrence of the birth, the greater the need for exactly dated events. The dates should be accurate to within a month.

If the margin of error for the birthtime is no more than thirty minutes, at least five dates are required. This is relatively easy to handle.

If the margin of error is greater — up to two hours — we require at least ten dates. Working with these is more time-consuming. And, for margins of error from two through a maximum twelve hours, the calculation has to be graphical. B. A. Mertz describes some very interesting possibilities for such cases in his book "Astrology as a Guide."[1]

Example Rectification

Here is an example of rectification where the uncertainty is 30 minutes. The woman whose chart appears in figure 30 had the following information to share:

When I was a girl some relatives teased me about my boyish appearance and behavior. My future stepmother was particularly cutting when she visited us for Christmas 1955.

When I was 18, my stepmother had her first child by my father (July 15, 1967). This interested me in becoming a children's nurse and I decided to enter training college. I did very well in the examination on March 15, 1968. College was really enjoyable and I felt very confident and self-reliant.

Easter Monday, 1969 (April 4, 1969), was the start of my first serious relationship with the opposite sex, and I married the man in question five years later (July 24, 1974). We lived together about two years, because shortly after the wedding I met the "man of my life." He and I did not get to know one another properly until the end of October 1974; though it would be more accurate to say that I got to know myself properly, because he was constantly analyzing me. These were the

---

[1]B. A. Mertz, *Astrologie als Wegweiser* (Stuttgart: Ebertin Verlag, 1982). This work is not available in English.

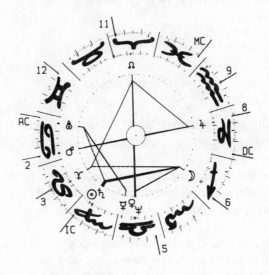

Figure 30. Female birth, August 31, 1949, between 0h00 and 0h30, Gurtnellen, Switzerland, 46°44N 8°40E. The chart was rectified so that the birthtime was determined to be 0h12m30s.

hardest years of my life, with many ups and downs plus the strain imposed on my "model marriage" by the pull of the new relationship.

From September through October, 1976, the heavily emotional separation brought me into conflict with my father: I was adamant over what I wanted to do and defied his patriarchal rule in the family. At this time I was already living with the man who is now my husband, and a year later, on October 3,1977, our unplanned first child arrived. The delivery was two weeks early; because I had overexerted myself at work and generally, and my water broke. The baby was very fine and delicate. Our second child was born February 16, 1981, and was a girl! She was deliberately conceived, and we knew from the start that a girl was on the way. Our wish was fulfilled.

The above statement had been pruned of everything except the data necessary for rectification.

Preliminaries

1) All the horoscope details are calculated for the central time in the range of possible birthtimes: in this case 0h15.

2) After the signs, planets, and aspects have been drawn in, cut around the outside of the zodiac circle to obtain a disk with the signs, planets and aspect configuration on it.

3) With a needle through its center, stick the disk onto a blank sheet of paper. The house cusps can now be entered on the paper while taking care that the disk does not slip. Afterward, the signs can be turned past the houses between the two MC positions.

4) In order to determine the limits within which the disk is to be turned, the MC has to be calculated for 0h00 and 0h30. Since the MC has a steady motion of 4° per 15 minutes, all that has to be done is to count 4° backward and forward from the calculated position of the MC. In the present instance, this means movements between 0°30′ and 8°30′ Pisces. This is the amount of play allowable for the possible Age Point aspects — which have to be calculated individually of course.

5) For this purpose, an AP-experience table is drawn up so that the necessary data can be seen at a glance during rectification work. Each experience is described in numbered chronological order in two or three key words. Additional columns give the dates and the house numbers. For example, the lady had a significant experience at age 19, and this falls in the 4th

house; another experience at age 34 falls in house 6. So we know where to find the Age Point. To make the calculations easier still, the size of each house can be shown.

6) The position of the Age Point must now be worked out for each date, as described in *Life Clock, Vol. 1*. The results are entered in the next column of the AP Experience Table.

7) In order to be able to enter the AP position correctly, we must give the MC its proper zodiac position, in this case 0°15′ Pisces. The AP marks must be placed on the blank sheet; just like the houses, the cusps of which show where the AP is on every 6th birthday.

Calculation of Aspect Positions

We start the rectification with the MC at 0°30′ Pisces and examine each of our nine AP positions in turn, asking ourselves which of them are in close conjunction or opposition to planets or have arrived at any of the cusps.

We turn the zodiac slowly and note significant positions of the AP arrow. With the MC = 1° Pisces, we are close to four such positions: AP 1 is in opposition to Jupiter, AP 2 is on the cusp of Virgo, AP 3 is 1° from the Sun, AP 6 is ½° from the cusp of Scorpio, and AP 9 is ½° away from the Moon. See figure 31 on page 182.

So we now have sufficient information to be able to test the hypothesis that MC = 1° Pisces. The aspects studied below are set out in a separate column of the AP experience table. The same method will be used for the second and third hypotheses.

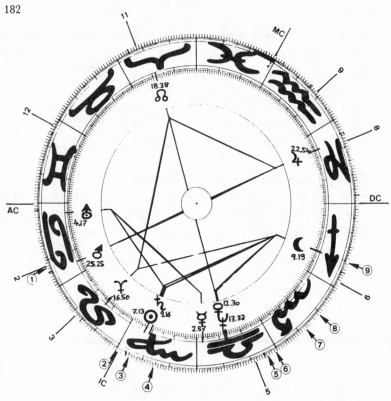

AP experience table (Birth Aug. 8, 1949, 46°44′ N 8°38′ E)				
AP No.	Brief description	Date	House No.	House size	Hypothesis AP aspects

AP No.	Brief description	Date	House No.	House size	Hypothesis AP aspects
1	Called a tomboy	24.12.55	2	29.8°	☍ ♃
2	Stepmother's first child	15. 7.67	3	19.2°	♌ / ♒
3	College exam.	15. 3.68	4	51.7°	✳ ☿ ~ ♂ ☉
4	1st man-friend	4. 4.69	4	51.7°	—
5	Marriage (in name)	24. 5.74	5	40.2°	~ □ ♂
6	2nd man-friend	22.10.74	5	40.2°	♎ / ♏
7	Divorce/quarrel with father	1.10.76	5	40.2°	⊻ ♀
8	1st child, son	3.10.77	5	40.2°	—
9	2nd child, daughter	16. 2.81	6	27.2°	♂ ☽
		MC degree used			1°00 ♓

Figure 31.   The MC at 1° Pisces.

1st Hypothesis

AP 1 = opposition Jupiter: the child was jeered at for being too boyish, and she resented this as unfair.

AP 2 = entry into Virgo, which contains a Sun-Saturn conjunction. Her divorced father gave her a stepmother and a half-brother.

AP 3 = sextile to Uranus and conjunction with the Sun: the young lady passed an important examination and became more self-confident.

AP 4 = no aspects at the 14th degree ± 1° tolerance.

AP 5 = at ca. 26° Libra; there is a square to Mars. This is rather too strong for a wedding that was not very important!

AP 6 = entry into intercepted Scorpio. The young woman met the man by whom she was later to have children. This AP is too weak!

AP 7 = semisextile to Venus: this would fit the divorce from the first husband but not the conflict with the father.

AP 8 = 1° after the aspect to the lunar node, but 4° before the next aspect, a sextile to Jupiter: the first child?

AP 9 = conjunction with the Moon at the birth of the wanted child.

Next the results have to be assessed. Only three of the aspects fit well: AP 1, 3, and 9. Poorer fits are Age Points 4, 6, and 8.

The time has now come to consider which of the nine experiences held most significance for this woman. One would expect that the birth of the first child and the initial romance with this child's father would coincide with prominent Age Point aspects. In addition, her divorce and the resulting dis-

pute with her father are very important, because this is where
she appears to have been able to break free from patriarchal
influences in general and to get her own way. Therefore we
need to give special weight to Age Points 6, 7 and 8. But there
is another point of considerable interest for chart interpretation. A little girl with such a Venus/Neptune/Moon formation
reaching out to the You and to the feminine Sun/Saturn com-
ponent in the 4th house would be very upset at a scolding for
being boyish! What was involved was her masculine side, for
which we must look to Mars. The latter is under great tension
on the 2nd cusp; and, what is more, it is in the region of AP 1.
So it looks as if it might be a good idea to turn the disk until AP
1 is in conjunction with Mars.

2nd Hypothesis

The MC of our new hypothesis is about 4° Pisces, and the new
Age Point aspects 1–9 immediately spring into view. See figure
32 on page 186.

AP 1 = conjunction Mars.

AP 2 = semisextile Mercury and sextile Uranus. The native's
mind receives new information giving rise to new, original
ideas. The experience of having a baby half-brother makes her
think, and she decides to teach in a kindergarten after graduat-
ing from college.

AP 3 = conjunction with the Sun and Saturn (possible mid-
point): passes entrance examination of teacher training
college.

AP 4 = semisextile to Pluto and quincunx to lunar node. A
fateful meeting led to what society saw as an ideal marriage.

AP 5 = marriage in the last half degree of Libra. The expectations of the family or group were fulfilled by the marriage.

AP 6 = making the acquaintance of the more compatible husband in the semisextile to Mercury followed by a trine to Uranus. The young woman writes in her biographical notes that this man was constantly analyzing her at the time, which fits in quite well with Uranus on the Ascendant — self-investigation!

AP 7 = $1/2°$ before the square to Pluto, which has only a blue aspect in the radical horoscope. Thus this is a significant new aspect, and it releases energetic forces of change: she defied her father and left the husband she had met at the semisextile to Pluto! (The second hypothesis gives us a cross-connection here.)

AP 8 = sextile to Jupiter, which is further linked to Mars. The first child is a boy — she could have had a very physical experience of motherhood, or had she now gained a role in society? Jupiter just before the 8th cusp.

AP 9 = sextile to Venus and also to Neptune. The planned child was a girl. She was conceived nine months earlier, when the AP was conjunct the Moon!

By and large, we can feel satisfied with our second hypothesis: APs 1, 3, and 5 are conjunctions or on the borders of signs, APs 2, 4, 6, 7 and 8 are new aspects for the planets concerned, and AP 9 is the fulfillment of a conjunction with the Moon, which means that in this case the conception of the child was more important than its birth, as far as the native was concerned (it was a planned child).

It is interesting, too, that she has mentioned nothing associated with the transiting of Mercury, Venus and Neptune. Now these three planets are the only ones near Low Points! Low Point periods are not readily recalled. Most of what is

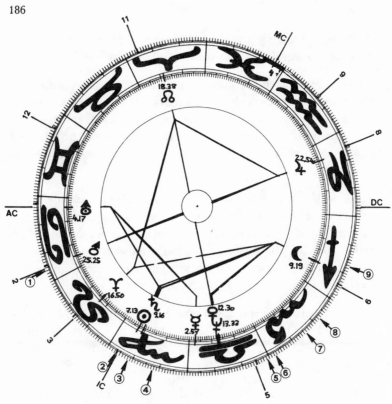

AP experience table (Birth Aug. 8, 1949, 46°44′ N 8°38′ E)				
AP No.	Brief description	Date	House No.	House size	2nd Hypothesis AP aspects
1	Called a tomboy	24.12.55	2	29.8°	♂ ♂
2	Stepmother's first child	15. 7.67	3	19.2°	⊻ ☿ ↔ ⚹ ☉̇
3	College exam.	15. 3.68	4	51.7°	♂ ☉ ↔ ♂ ♄
4	1st man-friend	4. 4.69	4	51.7°	⊻ ♈ ↔ ⊼ ☊
5	Marriage (in name)	24. 5.74	5	40.2°	29.5° ♎
6	2nd man-friend	22.10.74	5	40.2°	⊻ ☿ ↔ △ ☉̇
7	Divorce/quarrel with father	1.10.76	5	40.2°	□ ♈
8	1st child, son	3.10.77	5	40.2°	⚹ ♃
9	2nd child, daughter	16. 2.81	6	27.2°	⚹ ♀
		MC degree used		4°00 ♓	

Figure 32.   The MC at 4° Pisces.

experienced at such times happens inwardly. Wishes, ideals, missed opportunities, and guilt feelings can cloud the memory.

In spite of the gratifying results of the 2nd hypothesis, we shall test the remaining MC space through 8°30' Pisces in case there is another favorable position of the disk where the greatest possible number of AP arrows form interesting aspects.

3rd Hypothesis

The most fruitful position of the MC is 8° Pisces.

AP 1 = border between Cancer and Leo: first taste of patriarchal authority?

AP 2 = Conjunction with the Sun: the arrival of a baby half-brother gives more self-confidence.

AP 3 = semisextile to Venus: college entrance exam = femininity and harmony?

AP 4 = 1° before the trine to Jupiter.

AP 5 = semisextile to Mercury: marriage of the head rather than of the heart.

AP 6 = sextile to the Sun: meeting the second husband brought harmony to the self-awareness.

AP 7 = 20° Scorpio: no aspects within ± 2°!

AP 8 = 1° after the trine to Mars. The first child was a boy.

AP 9 = trine to Pluto. A personality ideal fulfilled in the second child.

Age Points 4, 7 and 8 do not supply exact aspects. The aspects for Age Point experiences 1, 2, 3, 6 and, truth to tell, 9 too, are unsatisfactory, especially from a psychological viewpoint. The motivations suggested by the aspects are too superficial, and the four most important experiences — 1, 6, 7 and 8 — make a very poor showing.

We shall dismiss this hypothesis; even though, with careful calculation, the aspects of APs 4, 7 and 8 could be given greater accuracy. Our intention is to find the proper time of birth on the basis of the 2nd hypothesis.

Fine Tuning of the 2nd Hypothesis

What we have to do now is to calculate the house system exactly, in order that the aspects made by the Age Point experiences are correct to within 10 minutes of arc. The first question requiring an answer is which, if any, of the nine events can be dated to the day. In fact there are several:

AP 1: because, in the full account of what happened, the visit of the aunt is said to have been on Christmas 1955, and this is what made the strongest impression = the conjunction with Mars.

AP 4: the meeting with the first husband was on Easter Monday 1969 = the link between the semisextile to Pluto and the quincunx to the Moon's North Node.

AP 8: With the birth of the first child, personal freedom was reduced and material existence gained a new perspective = sextile to Jupiter (new aspect!).

Our calculations will be based on AP 8, using AP 1 as a control.

Calculation of the Corrected House System

The starting point can be formulated as follows: Jupiter at 22°54′ Capricorn is sextile to 22°54′ Scorpio, the position of AP 8. In addition, we have one more known quantity: the time span separating the event from the 5th cusp or 24th birthday, August 8, 1973. This time span "Z" is the difference between October 3, 1977, and August 3, 1973 = 4 years, 1 month and ca. 3 days. Using the AP table and the house size (5th = 40°10′) we convert "Z" into the corresponding degree distance "X," which is then subtracted from the fixed AP position. The formula for the calculation is in two parts as follows:

1) HS° divided by 6 years and multiplied by Z years
   = X°.

2) AP° − X° = HC°.

A pocket calculator simplifies the arithmetic, which looks like this: 40.167° divided by 6 (years) and then multiplied by 4.086 (years) = 27.35°, or 27°21′. Now the AP position is smaller (22°54′), so we must first add 30° (of Libra) before we can subtract "X," 22°54′ Scorpio + 30° = 52°54′ Libra − 27°21′ = 25°33′ Libra.

This result is the 5th cusp, and by referring to the table of houses we can discover the MC and the other other cusps.

Opening the table of houses to the MC in Pisces, we look for 11th/5th houses cusp 25°33′ at N. Lat. 47°, and find that the nearest to it is 26°05′ under MC 4°. See figure 33 on page 190.

However, the birth place is at 46°44′ north latitude. That is to say, it is at a certain proportional distance between 46 and 47 degrees of latitude; to be precise, at a forty-four sixtieth from 46°. In decimals, 44/60 = 0.733. We now take the degree difference between the 9/5 cusps for 46° and 47° north latitude and multiply it by this factor. The difference is 26°05′ − 24°55′ = 1°10′, and 1°10′ × 0.73 = 51′. This is 44/60 of the 5th

22ʰ 23ᵐ 35ˢ		M 4° ✕	335° 53' 38''			22ʰ 27ᵐ 21ˢ		M 5° ✕	336° 50' 21''	
XI	XII	A	II	III	N LAT	XI	XII	A	II	III
22 52	2 39	♋ 0 37	23 06	13 43	44°	24 06	3 39	1 28	23 57	14 37
23 51	3 46	1 27	23 40	14 00	45°	25 05	4 45	2 18	24 30	14 54
24 55	4 57	2 21	24 15	14 18	46°	26 10	5 56	3 11	25 05	15 12
26 05	6 11	3 16	24 50	14 36	47°	27 20	7 10	4 06	25 40	15 30
27 20	7 31	4 13	25 27	14 54	48°	28 35	8 29	5 03	26 17	15 48
♈28 42	8 54	5 12	26 05	15 13	49°	♈29 58	9 51	6 01	26 55	16 06
♉ 0 13	10 22	6 13	26 44	15 32	50°	♉ 1 28	11 18	7 02	27 33	16 26
1 54	11 55	7 17	27 24	15 52	51°	3 09	12 50	8 05	28 13	16 45

Figure 33.   An extract from *Tables of Houses* by Dr. Walter Koch and E. Schaeck.

cusp of 46° N. Lat. So if we add 51' to the cusp value for 46°, we obtain the exact 5th house cusp for MC 4° Pisces: 24°55' + 51' = 25°46' Libra. The deviation from the required value is so slight that we can treat the MC as if it were exactly 4°Pisces.

As a control, we shall examine AP 1, for which purpose we need to know the size of the 2nd house as given under our newly established MC between 46° and 47° N. Lat. The distance between cusps 2 and 3 is 20°03' at 40°N. Lat., and only 19°46' at 47° N. Lat. For calculating the monthly motion of the AP, it is sufficient to use a house size of 20°; in which case the AP moves through the 2nd house at a rate of 16'40'' per month. The time gap between AP 1 and the 6th birthday (2nd cusp) is four months, so the AP is 4 × 16.7 = 66.8' from the 2nd cusp.

The latter is at 24°35' Cancer (by interpolation), and by adding the degree distance from AP 1, we obtain the AP position 25°42' Cancer. Mars is posited at 25°25' Cancer, therefore the AP transited it 17' earlier. Since this transit has already been found to be extremely precise, we ought in theory to move the MC back a little to 3°50' Pisces.

In the tables of houses, local sidereal time (LST) is given at top left above the MC. But we have reduced MC 4° Pisces by 10'. Now, when the MC travels 60' = 1°, the LST changes by 226 sec.! So the reduction by 10' amounts to 226 s. ÷ 6 = 38 s., which has to be subtracted from the LST: 22h23m35s – 38s is exactly 22h22m57s.

To rectify the time of birth, all we need is the difference between the local sidereal time for 0h15 and the corrected LST: 22h25m27s – 22h22m57s = 0h02m30s. The corrected LST is smaller, so the time of birth is 2.5 minutes earlier than 0h15. The rectified, exact time of birth is 0h12m30s.

Bibliography

Arroyo, Stephen. *Astrology, Psychology & The Four Elements.* Sebastopol, CA: CRCS, 1975.

Assagioli, Roberto. *The Act of Will.* New York: Penguin, 1974.

Bailey, Alice A. *Esoteric Astrology,* Vol. 3 of *A Treatise on the Seven Rays.* New York: Lucis Publishing Company, 1975.

Brunton, Paul. *Quest of the Overself.* York Beach, ME: Samuel Weiser, 1984.

Durckheim, Karlfied Graf. *Vom doppelten Ursprung des Menchen.* Herder-Verlag, 1973.

Goethe, J. W. *Essays on Art and Literature,* Vol. 3 of *Goethe's Collected Works.* New York: Suhrkamp, 1986.

Huber, Bruno and Louise, *The Astrological Houses: A Psychological View of Man and His World.* York Beach, ME: Samuel Weiser, 1984.

_____. *Life Clock: Age Progression in the Horoscope,* Vol. 1, 1982; Vol. 2, 1986. York Beach, ME: Samuel Weiser.

Huber, Louise. *Reflections and Meditations on the Signs of the Zodiac.* Tempe, AZ: American Federation of Astrologers, 1984.

Itten, Johannes. *The Art of Color.* New York: Van Nostrand Reinhold, 1974.

Jung, C. G. *Memories, Dreams, Reflections,* ed. by Aniela Jaffe. New York: Random House, Pantheon Books, 1963.

Kandinsky, Wassily. *Concerning the Spiritual in Art.* New York: Dover, 1977.

Krishnamurti, Jiddu. *Freedom from the Known*. New York: Harper & Row, 1975.

Levinson, Daniel J. *The Seasons of a Man's Life*. New York: Knopf, 1978.

Lüscher, Max. *Lüscher Color Test*. New York: Simon and Schuster, Pocket Books, 1980.

Müller, Aemilius. *Die moderne Farbenharmonielehre*. Winterthur: Chromos-Verlag, 1959.

Newton, Isaak. *Opticks, or a Treatise of the Reflections, Refractions, Inflections & Colours of Light*. Magnolia, MA: Peter Smith.

Ostwald, Wilhelm. *Die Farbenlehre*. (div. Abhandlungen), Leipzig, 1912–1923.

Stern, Paul. *C. G. Jung: Prophet des Unbewussten*. Munich: Piper, 1977.

About the Authors

Bruno and Louise Huber are the founders of the internation-
ally recognized Swiss astrology school, Astro-Psychology Institute, in Zurich. They now also have a school in Devon,
England, the English Huber School. In addition to a personal
counseling practice, they teach at both institutes in Switzerland
and England, and lecture throughout the world. Both have
been keynote speakers at the American Federation of Astrologers Convention for the past several conferences, and they host
the now-famous international World Congress in astrology at
Lucerne, Switzerland. From 1958 until 1960 they studied with
Dr. Roberto Assagioli, founder of psychosynthesis, in Flor-
ence, Italy. The Hubers have been working with astrological
psychology in teaching and counseling for over 30 years.